***Enneagram* (*ANY uh gram*)**

A system for identifying the nine personality types: Perfectionist, Nurturer, Achiever, Romantic, Observer, Skeptic, Adventurer, Leader, and Peacemaker

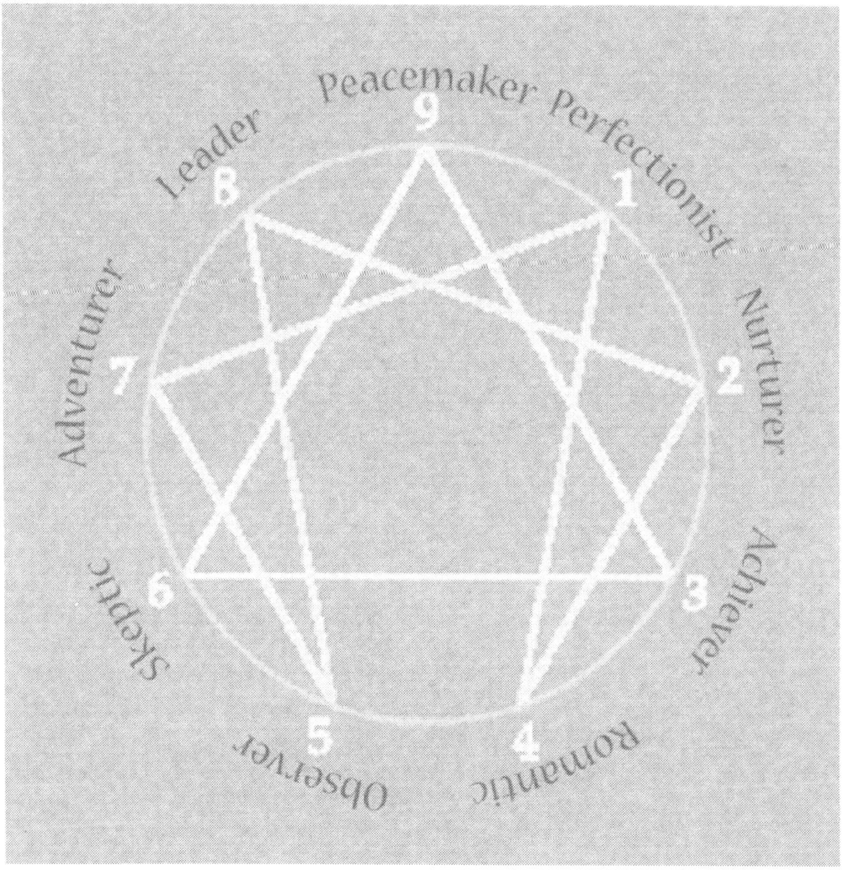

BELIEVABLE CHARACTERS: *CREATING WITH ENNEAGRAMS*

by Laurie Schnebly

First Edition

Published by
Cider Press
2641 N. Arcadia
Tucson AZ 85712
USA
CiderPressBooks@yahoo.com

ISBN 0-930831-03-9

Cover Design: Penny Skubal

Contact the author at
www.BookLaurie.com

Writers sometimes ask, "What personality type would my FBI agent be?"

That's where enneagrams come in handy.

We can assume that an FBI agent believes in law and order, but that's not nearly enough to define a character.

The agent might live with a wife and kids, or a dog, or a crotchety uncle, but that's still not enough to define his character.

We might know his birthplace, his parents' occupations, his siblings' names and his favorite childhood pet, but we're still just scratching the surface.

It's when we get to his enneagram type that some real clues to this FBI agent's personality begin to emerge.

CONTENTS

To my FairyDust friends

Allison Davidson
Lois Faye Dyer
Christine Flynn
Patricia Kay
Julia Mozingo
Cheryl Reavis
Myrna Temte

who share the everyday life
of writing with such humor,
compassion and joy

and to the many writers whose
participation in my
"Creating Your Hero's Fatal Flaw" workshops
yielded such wonderful material

Thank you all.

INTRODUCTION

Every writer wants the same thing.

Or maybe several of the same things, like a spot on the *New York Times* best-seller list or a front-aisle display in the neighborhood bookstore or fan letters saying "you changed my life," but every writer shares one special goal.

Memorable characters.

Think about the characters you remember. They were probably the people responsible for your favorite book. Most of us writers have a few dozen best-loved books, and in almost every case they're favorites because of the characters.

So of course we want to create people our readers will remember. Maybe not fondly, not if they're someone like Hannibal Lecter or Inspector Javert, but our characters don't need to be loved.

Just remembered.

How can we make that happen?

Psychological Tools

Psychological tools bring to mind visions of the ink-blot test, or Pavlov's dogs salivating at the sound of a bell. Those aren't the kind of tools writers need.

What we need are the tools used by counselors and human resources people to determine what someone is *really* like.

Then, unlike the counselors and human resources people, we get to use our knowledge of these people to – well, to ruin their lives.

Or at least put them in serious trouble. Like watching the love of their life marry some insipid cousin before heading off to the Civil War. The chance to achieve a dream, but at the cost of breaking a vow. Their sworn enemy given the power to confiscate the land they love. Something that anyone would agree means a difficult time ahead.

Because without that risk of failure, there's not going to be much of a book. If everything around them stays rosy, these characters aren't going to have any chance to grow or learn or change their personality. They won't face any kind of trouble that'll keep the reader turning pages until three in the morning.

Of course, *any* characters can wind up in trouble if a plane crashes into their house. Or if their village is invaded by barbarians. Even so, imagine how barbarian invaders would affect Scarlett O'Hara and Sherlock Holmes.

Two different stories, right?

Because of the characters' personalities.

There are dozens, maybe hundreds, of ways to choose a character's personality. Every writer builds an individual toolbox of the methods they find most helpful. And a lot of writers have found one tool particularly helpful:

Enneagrams

"Ennea" is the Greek word for nine, so you can guess how many personality types are in the enneagram system. It comes from the Sufi culture and was brought west by G. Ivanovich Gurdjieff around a century ago.

In a way it's comparable to astrology, which defines twelve personality types. But enneagrams are even more convenient, because they represent psychological types every reader can believe in...and every writer can use.

That's partly because we all have *each* of the nine types within ourselves. Everyone has experienced what it's like to be a Type **One, a Perfectionist**, concerned with getting something done right. You might have done that just this morning, observing the speed limit even though there was nobody in sight. Or last week, writing a letter to the editor about why your city needs better crosswalks.

You've been a Type **Two, a Nurturer**, as well. Maybe when you tucked your kids in bed and vowed to cherish every moment of how precious they are. When you saw a neighbor choking back tears and immediately asked what was wrong.

Last time you were a Type **Three, an Achiever**, might have been when you finished a report with a glow of satisfaction in knowing that your work was outstanding. Or when you dressed up for a special evening and realized that you looked really, really good.

As a Type **Four, a Romantic**, you've felt big, vast sweeping emotions at the end of a blockbuster movie. Or when someone you thought of as a dear friend betrayed you, leaving you abandoned and aghast and shaken to the core.

You've been a **Five, an Observer**, when you got engrossed in a term paper and scrambled intensely through a stack of books for just the right quote. Maybe you spent an entire weekend wrapped up in the study of something that absolutely fascinated you.

You've been a **Six, a Skeptic**, when you found yourself questioning the wisdom of a situation others took for granted. Could you really feel safe eating a hamburger with Mad Cow Disease on the rise? Was the rust on that fire extinguisher a bad sign?

As a **Seven, an Adventurer**, you've delighted in a spontaneous walk in the rain or an impulsive stop at a new restaurant. You might have enjoyed planning a trip to India, thinking up names for a cutting-edge business, or dreaming of a best-selling screenplay.

When you saw someone being treated unfairly and spoke up about it, you were an **Eight, a Leader**. You've seen how things should be handled and taken action to make certain they're done, that people who need care and protection are assured of getting it.

And as a **Nine, a Peacemaker**, you've seen both sides of a question. You've acknowledged the value and worth of several different viewpoints, refraining from imposing your own on those around you, and helping people reach a consensus.

Maybe you haven't experienced every single one of those situations. But you've definitely felt at least two or three...and likely a lot more than that.

> **All of us have elements of all nine types within our own personalities. Some of those types feel more comfortable and more familiar than others. Whichever one of them is the *most* true, the most frequent, is your enneagram type.**

And the same holds true for your characters.

Sometimes people can spot their type just from a brief description like those above. Other times it helps to take a quiz like those in the next nine chapters. What matters most for writers, though, is that each of the nine types offers a starting place for building a character whose personality will create enough genuine conflict to keep the story interesting.

Once you've identified your characters' types, you can see how they'll interact with the world and with themselves – and where they're most likely to encounter problems that make for great fiction.

Challenging Characters

If a character has no problems, there's not much reason to keep reading. (An exception might be stories for very young children, where a trip to the mailbox while examining flowers along the way can be utterly captivating.)

But most readers want to see characters facing some kind of challenge. Barbarian invaders are fine. So are a flat tire, a lost contract or a lost child. So are global warming, a rained-out picnic, or the awareness that Mom always liked Younger Brother best.

Problems are the only thing that give characters a chance to learn and grow and change.

And those problems can come from within the characters, such as resentment of Younger Brother, or from something completely beyond their control – say, a brick falling off the roof just as they walk below it. That's where we get Internal and External conflict.

External conflict comes from the situation at hand, like the corporate takeover or the kidnapped child or the Civil War raiders. *Internal* conflict is what keeps your characters from being perfectly happy within themselves. (Because if you have a hero who's completely satisfied with himself and his life from page 1 on, then completely satisfied with his boss and his family and his neighbors from pages 2, 3 and 4 on…well, you won't have much of a novel.) For an engrossing story, you've got to have conflict. You've got to ruin these people's lives!

Since I come from a counseling psychology perspective, that's where I look for the conflict. Confederate vs. Yankee is fine, there's nothing wrong with that. But what *is* it, within your various characters' personalities, that keeps them from living happily ever after with themselves and everyone else around them? That's what makes your story fascinating.

There are all kinds of opportunities for external conflict *between* characters and internal conflict *within* characters, and all these conflicts will keep readers involved. But no matter what causes the trouble, it's safe to say that conflict comes from personality.

Because even if the problem is a randomly falling brick, your characters' personalities will make a huge difference in how they react to it.

Spotting Personality Types

Whether you're creating a brand-new character from scratch, or identifying a character who already exists, the quiz that begins each of the next nine chapters will help you determine which type your character is.

Enneagram tradition, by the way, says that nobody is allowed to tell anyone else their type. So if I read about the Eight and realize it sounds just like my husband, I can't put down the book and say, "Hey, Pete, you're an Eight." Only *he* can determine that he's an Eight...or a Six, or a Three, or whatever.

But as writers, we're exempt from that tradition. We can make our characters whatever type we want!

If you take the quiz on behalf of a character (or even on behalf of yourself or someone you know) and wind up with several options all scoring equally high, that's okay.

Reading about each type will make it easier to narrow down the top-scoring contenders and decide which seems the most valid. If traits from several different types *all* seem like part of this person's character, the fact is that they probably are.

Here's why:

Wings & Connections

Now we're getting into some technical stuff, but it's not all that bad – even for writers who tend to be better with words than numbers.

The idea is, each type takes on traits of the numbers next to its own. So if you're a Nine, you'll also have some traits of an Eight and a One. Those are called "wings."

Each type also shares traits of two additional types, which are all over the map. Enneagram theorists say that each type "goes to" two others, and the diagram shows you where they go.

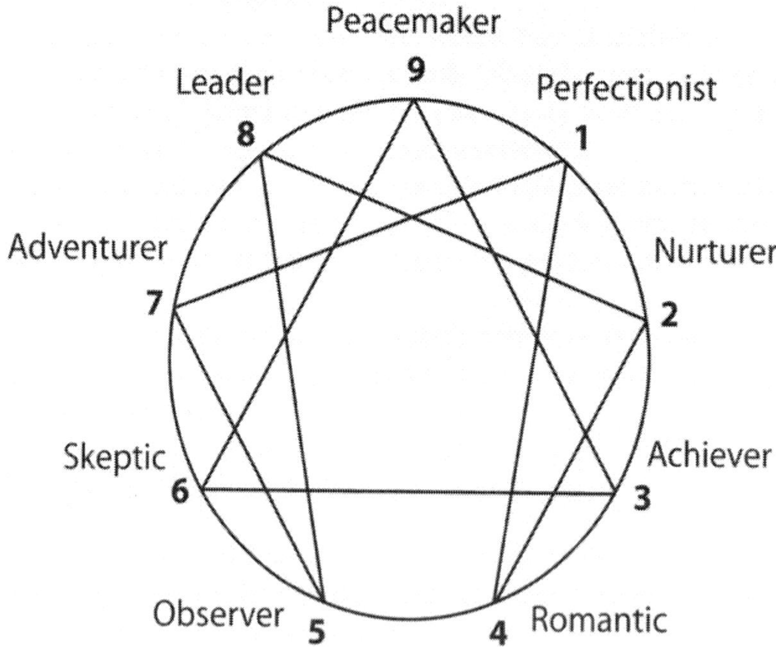

So let's take my Type Eight husband, look at his number on the chart, and we can see that he goes to Two and Five. That means he shares some of their traits as well as those in his Seven and Nine wings.

Some theorists say that people "go to" one type when they're stressed, and another when they're healthy, but others say both types can be good or bad. And as writers, we can use whatever theory will give us the most compelling characters.

But since each type's wings and connections may be more detail than you want, they're covered in the appendix on page 216.

Subtypes

Another factor that gives us so many choices is that each of the nine types has three subtypes. For example, take a look at Greta Garbo and Sherlock Holmes. Both are Fives, but you'd never mistake one for the other if you met them on the street. (Or to be fair, let's say your only contact was via email. It'd still be pretty hard to get Sherlock and Greta mixed up.)

The subtypes reflect where a person directs the most energy – toward self-preservation, one-on-one relationships, or their entire social group.

We all value all three in different amounts. When you're holed up studying for the final exam, that's your Self-Preservation subtype in action. When you're on a lunch date talking for hours, that's your Intimacy subtype. And when you're in a crowd of fans all cheering for the home team, that's your Social subtype.

Ideally they're each weighted equally, but most of us tend to lean more toward one area than toward the others. That area will be a source of great strength in our lives because we're good at it, but it can also be a source of great weakness because we've left the other areas alone.

Still, great weakness is a fine thing when it comes to building characters!

Any of these three subtypes can get a character in trouble, creating conflict either *within* this person or *between* the person and someone else. So how do the subtypes work?

Self-Preservation

People in this subtype are concerned with exactly that: individual self-preservation. Do they have enough batteries in the smoke alarm? How can they afford their kid's tuition? Is there anywhere they can get some privacy? They're concerned with basic survival issues...survival of the body or the spirit or both.

If they were stranded on a desert island with plenty of survival gear, they'd be fine by themselves.

So you can imagine the potential conflict when these people feel some threat toward self-preservation, either from another person or from the situation at hand. Whether the problem comes from within themselves or from the outside, it's going to create conflict for this subtype.

Intimacy

People in this subtype are the most concerned with one-on-one relationships...not just a lover, but every individual friendship. They want to spend time alone with everyone they care about, just the two of them, talking as intimately as they can. "What's going on? How're you feeling? Here's what's new with me."

If they were on that desert island, they'd want only one other person with them...someone who'd be just as involved with the relationship as they are.

It's easy to envision a relationship in which both characters are the Intimacy subtype, and how little conflict that would generate. But in fact, there can still be conflict. Suppose Juliet has spent all afternoon preparing a romantic dinner for two, just before Romeo gets a desperate call from his lonely, widowed mother asking if he has time to talk. Two people sharing the same subtype is no guarantee of a conflict-free life.

Social

This subtype is concerned with the community as a whole, with what's going on in their entire group. That group might be their church, their co-workers, their extended family...whatever it is, these people love being part of the group. They want their whole gang on that desert island, and they want to do their part for the whole social structure.

That was the problem in *Animal Farm*, where various animals had their own ideas of what was best for the community. That was the problem in *Bridge On The River Kwai*, where the American and the Japanese leaders each saw the value of their group as a high priority.

It can also be a problem when the Social character puts more emphasis on the group, while the Self-Preservation or Intimacy character puts more emphasis somewhere else.

None of these subtypes is right or wrong, but they all offer wonderful opportunities for conflict.

Fortunately for us writers, conflict is what offers the chance for growth. Because growth *has* to happen for these characters to reach their happy ending.

Now, one way for growth to happen is that people can learn to compromise (like Romeo and Juliet, who might agree to invite Mom for dinner and postpone their romantic evening until she's safely asleep).

And of course compromise is a good step toward resolving conflict between characters.

But what about within characters?

The most interesting books are those where the main characters overcome something within themselves.

It's fascinating to watch, and it gives our readers something to root for in addition to rescuing the hiker or catching the criminal or marching down the aisle or finding the treasure. All perfectly valid endings in their own right, but they're enhanced when the character has achieved some individual growth as well.

Yet this kind of growth can't happen unless people have something they need to overcome. And all of our memorable characters need to overcome something…no matter what their type or subtype.

Which Is Best?

People sometimes think that one subtype is ideal, and the others are second-rate. Sometimes they think one of the nine types is better than the other eight.

Not true.

It's hard to imagine God saying, "I'm going to make a handful of wonderful people, and they're all going to be Ones. Then we'll have those scuddy Twos and those loser Threes...."

Every type is valuable. Every type has tremendous assets and strengths and capabilities, which we'll see spelled out in the next nine chapters. Every type can be a truly heroic character, whom readers will love and root for and wish they could meet for dinner.

And, luckily for us writers, every type can *also* have some character defects that range from the mildly annoying to the truly appalling. When we're writing great drama, we can call those traits their "fatal flaws."

Every character type has a fatal flaw. These major or minor defects of character – or (to put a more positive spin on it) these Opportunities For Growth – are a wonderful thing for writers who want to create a compelling book.

If you're writing a book where things turn out well, it's likely that your characters will overcome their fatal flaws in time for a happy ending. If you're writing a tragedy, they probably won't.

But either way, the flaws don't need to be fatal.

Still, some writers are bothered by the idea of characters with *any* kind of a flaw. "I write about good people who love their children and pay their taxes and mow their lawns," a friend protests. "These characters don't need some personality defect dragging them down!"

Of course not.

Look at James Bond.

Look at Barbie and Ken.

Look at the Seven Dwarfs.

They all do just fine as characters.

But nobody has ever mistaken them for real-life people.

Real-life people *have* flaws. Most of them work to overcome their worst defects, which is why we're able to live with our roommates and neighbors and co-workers instead of retreating to some Tibetan cave.

But it's those defects, or the desire to overcome them, which can lead to our characters' motivation.

Motivation

The fact is, virtually everyone is doing the best they can with what they've got.

A serial killer? Yep. A cheating spouse? Yep. A compulsive spender? Yep.

As writers, we can make those people every bit as easy to understand as the tax-paying, lawn-mowing, child-loving characters. (Maybe they're one and the same.) That doesn't surprise anyone who knows that even the darkest villains have some plausible motivation for whatever they do.

None of us ever does *anything* without a reason. If you just crossed your legs, you had a reason: your body was uncomfortable in the old position. If you move to Antarctica, you have a reason: maybe you got a job there, or someone you love got a job there and you'd rather be with this person in Antarctica than without them somewhere else.

We don't always think about our reasons for whatever we do, but no matter what we do, there's a reason.

So all our characters, just like all real-life people, are doing whatever they think will work best for them at this point in their life. Holing up in an ivory tower. Partying all night. Nurturing everyone they can get their hands on. Worrying about terrorism. Everyone picks what seems like the best way of getting along in the world.

Whether cooperating with others or clashing with them, being friendly or being withdrawn, angry or cheerful, early or late, tidy or sloppy...whatever we do, we do it for a reason.

Of course, we don't always agree with other people's choices. My husband thinks we get better service from lazy waiters if he glares at them; I think we get better service if I beam at them. But glaring or beaming, we both have a reason for what we do.

And so do our characters. They might not understand other people's reasons, or even their own, but it's rarely a case of one character being completely right and everyone else being completely wrong.

We don't care much about the cabbie who drives our detective character to the train station, so this cabbie doesn't need any special motivation. This character doesn't need any fatal flaws. Nor does he need to overcome any problems in his life or his personality.

But every major character has to overcome something in order to grow and evolve during the course of the book. And that's why writers need to know our characters' fatal flaws.

Fatal Flaws

It's handy that enneagram theorists have already identified a flaw for each of the nine personality types.

Those names come straight from the list of Seven Deadly Sins. (Although because the math was slightly off, they had to make up two flaws that never made it onto the Biblical list.)

For enneagram personalities, the nine fatal flaws are:

Perfectionist One	–	**anger**
Nurturer Two	–	**pride**
Achiever Three	–	**deception**
Romantic Four	–	**envy**
Observer Five	–	**avarice**
Skeptic Six	–	**fear**
Adventurer Seven	–	**gluttony**
Leader Eight	–	**lust**
Peacemaker Nine	–	**sloth**

And even though each flaw is assigned to a particular type, *any* type could commit *any* of those sins at any time.

For instance, even though Anger is the fatal flaw of a One, a character who gets angry when somebody murders her husband isn't necessarily a One. A Two's weakness is Pride, but any character might feel pride under the right circumstances.

So if you already know that your hero's fatal flaw is envy, that doesn't necessarily make him a Four. If you know your hero *is* a

Four, it's logical that there will be times when he struggles with envy…but there may also be times when he struggles with anger, pride and other weaknesses.

Regardless of a person's weakness, most people have had plenty of practice in compensating for their flaws. Not only those which plague their own type, but plenty of others as well! If I notice the call of gluttony whenever I drive past a Krispy Kreme stand, it's a pretty safe bet that I've learned to ignore that call – at least some of the time.

The same is true of any character flaw. If you spot one that belongs to your own type, chances are you've already managed to overcome it most of the time. The world is full of people who get along pretty well in everyday life, and that's because we all grow and learn and adapt to minimize our flaws.

But stress can bring out the worst in people. Stress, or conflict, is what keeps a story interesting. So our characters are going to come up against situations that reveal the worst of their flaws… which will give them the opportunity for a triumphant change.

No matter which type they are.

And that leads to a common question:

What Type Is *This* Character?

Every time I give a workshop on enneagrams, some writer will ask a question along the lines of:

"I'm writing about an FBI agent. Which of the types would he be?"

It's gotten so that, if nobody asks this question, I ask it myself. Because the answer is so important, it'd make a great slogan for using enneagrams to create characters:

Your FBI agent could be any one of the nine types. It all depends on what kind of person you want him to be.

We can assume that an FBI agent believes in law and order, but that's not nearly enough to define a character.

The agent might live with a wife and kids, or a dog, or a crotchety uncle, but that's still not enough to define his character.

We might know his birthplace, his parents' occupations, his siblings' names and his favorite childhood pet, but we're still just scratching the surface.

It's when we get to his enneagram type that some real clues to this FBI agent's personality begin to emerge.

As a One, for instance, he's all about upholding what's Right & Good.

As a Two, his top priority is the people he's caring for.

As a Three, it's giving the best possible performance.

As a Four, he's keenly aware of the emotional nuances of any situation.

As a Five, he's fascinated with the investigative process.

As a Six, his concern is preserving security.

As a Seven, it's fully experiencing every new situation.

As an Eight, he wants to protect the innocent in an unjust world.

As a Nine, he wants to maintain peace and tranquility wherever possible.

Each of those personalities could describe either a highly successful, competent FBI agent...or, if the story requires it, a failure at any FBI mission.

So knowing a character's career doesn't necessarily provide much of a clue to the character's enneagram type.

But the following chapters will.

How This Works

Each chapter starts with a quiz that can help identify a prospective character's most likely types. Sometimes one type is clearly the winner; other times there are several possibilities.

Information on each type's own strengths and weaknesses, childhood, work style and relationships will narrow it down even further.

And to show how each character type operates, we'll see each type starring in imaginary scenes from books of various genres.

The scenes feature:

- A cop tracking the blackmailer who's threatening his beloved daughter's arrogant father-in-law.
- A princess who has to save the kingdom by allying with either the vampire lord or the rebel dragon-rider.
- A solitary cowboy fighting off the cattle rustlers who've been decimating his herd.
- A teenager whose only friend finds treasure buried in the family's backyard.
- A career woman who hires a detective to find the baby she gave up for adoption 13 years ago.

All five characters will face different conflicts in each of the following chapters, depending on their enneagram type.

So let's see how to put *our* enneagram-type characters into situations that will keep readers turning pages all night long.

CHAPTER ONE

QUIZ

- ☐ Do you like being well organized?
- ☐ Do you generally keep your word?
- ☐ Do you feel irritated when people break rules?
- ☐ Do you sometimes think of yourself as judgmental?
- ☐ Do you have a strong inner sense of "the right way" to do things?
- ☐ Are you almost always punctual?
- ☐ Is perfection important to you?
- ☐ Do you worry about being judged or criticized?
- ☐ Do you find it hard to forgive when someone has wronged you?
- ☐ Do you often do more than your fair share?

___ **TOTAL FOR ONE**

TYPE ONE:
The Perfectionist, The Reformer

Suppose you want a role model to teach children right from wrong. Or a judge to determine the difference between true and false intentions. Or a philosopher to create a code of ethics for upholding the common good.

There's nobody better than a One.

Ones have a keen sense of right and wrong, and they're determined to stay on the side of good. They believe in making the world a better place, in working toward perfection, in avoiding mistakes.

So every One is either a pillar of virtue who makes the world better by hard work and dedication to what's right, or a nuisance to those who don't share the same ethic.

In old Western movies, where there are clear boundaries between the good guys in the white hats and the bad guys in the black hats, the Ones always wear white.

They're the people who genuinely believe in truth and justice for all. They'll do their best to live up to what's right, even when it costs them – if they've promised to weed Aunt Mary's garden on Saturday morning, they'll be there.

Even if it means cutting short an evening with The Love Of Their Life on Friday night, they'll show up at the garden. "I gave my word," the One will explain. "Just because I'm having the best time of my life doesn't make it right to go back on a promise."

You've got to admire integrity like that. Especially because such Ones aren't just putting on a good show. They truly *believe* in upholding what's right, in doing what's fair, in keeping their word and following the rules and making the world a better place. It's not just talk; it's action.

Since they're good at seeing things in black and white, Ones don't believe in gray areas. Slippery evasions might work for some people, but a One knows that either something is right or it's wrong. None of this lazy middle-ground stuff; none of these last-minute exceptions. Even if they'd like to cut themselves some slack occasionally, they know better. The idea of doing your duty means that you're always on duty. No ifs, ands or buts.

If a One ever *does* slip up, you can bet the self-criticism will be harsh. "How could I have done that? I'm supposed to know better!" Forgiveness is hard, because they have such high standards for the entire world.

Including themselves.

It's that solid moral compass which makes Ones their own toughest critic.

They'll do whatever it takes to avoid such criticism – which means they won't take any action they can't justify wholeheartedly. They set up rules for themselves, and make a point of living by those rules.

If they're surrounded by people who preach the value of taking time for fun or forgiving oneself for errors, Ones may incorporate that philosophy into their own set of rules. But they'll put a very black-and-white spin on it: "Remember, you *must* make time for fun." "Remember, you *must* be ready to forgive yourself as soon as you've atoned for an error."

You can see how these crusading Ones rarely get to put down the burden of Good Behavior. They're constantly working toward perfection, constantly trying to become the best they can be. It can become a little compulsive, this attempt to avoid any mistakes, and Ones can get furious whenever someone makes a mistake. Especially when it's the One.

But since anger isn't a "good" emotion, Ones are likely to deny that they feel any anger. After all, losing control of emotions is a "bad" thing. And bad things must be avoided.

So instead, they focus on what they do best. Good, solid, honest, hard work. Practicality. Independence. Community service. Putting the family first. The kind of values we associate with hardy ancestors, the kind that we take pride in passing down to future generations. For a One, there's no other way to live.

Ever.

Famous Ones

While other types become famous in the arts or in business, a large number of Ones achieve greatness in the area of social service. Whether it's religion, government or journalism, Ones have a knack for focusing attention on how to make the world a better place.

Look at Pope John Paul II. Martin Luther, Sir Thomas More, Nelson Mandela, César Chávez. All of them crusaded for a better world, along whatever lines they believed in, and were devoted to improving the lot of humanity.

Moving from the worldwide arena to American politics and law, we find still more Ones making a point to stand up for what's right.

They may draw criticism from those who disagree with their position, but that doesn't change their determination to work for what they believe in.

Look at Hillary Clinton and Thurgood Marshall. Harry Truman and Ralph Nader. Sandra Day O'Connor and Barry Goldwater. Nobody would group any of them into similar political camps, but they all illustrate the One's dedication to working for a world that lives up to its potential.

That's true no matter where a One calls home. Margaret Thatcher, St. Augustine and Alexander Solzhenitsyn show the same determination. And speaking of writers, we see a One-like dedication to improvement in the work of George Bernard Shaw, Mark Twain, William F. Buckley and Arthur Miller.

Of course, performers can embody that belief in a greater good as well. Gregory Peck, Katharine Hepburn and Charlton Heston routinely played Ones. And on TV, we've seen it in news people like Peter Jennings, Ted Koppel and Tom Brokaw...anyone who believes in making the world a better place.

One's Heroic Strengths

Ones make wonderful heroes in the world of Good Vs. Evil, because they're so firmly on the side of Good. Their integrity is beyond question, and anybody who knows a One won't be surprised by this habit of always doing what's right.

Not that it's necessarily easy. But Ones don't ask for life to be easy. They just want the opportunity to live up to the highest standards, to do right and think right and *be* right.

Since their vision is rarely clouded by questions of morality – there *is* no question; they *know* what's right – they're good at viewing the world with an objective eye.

Among a crew of desert island survivors, it's likely the One who'd be asked to judge any disputes that arise. Ones are known for their dispassionate discernment, their fair-mindedness, and their willingness to consider every fact when it comes to judging right from wrong.

There's also no danger of a One ever accepting a bribe. Ever letting down the team. Ever refusing a fair share of the work. And the most heroic Ones temper their idealism with realism. Knowing that not everyone can sustain their own high standards, they lead by example rather than by edict.

Such a leader embodies the traits every reader expects of a true hero. Utterly selfless. Willing to sacrifice personal good for the greater principle. High ideals, but respectful of others…such as the small-town minister who acknowledges that the local rabbi and priest have equally valuable insights.

If you're envisioning this character with a glow of righteousness streaming from overhead, you're probably right on target!

One's Fatal Flaws

That glow of righteousness can lead to problems, of course, and you can see how most Ones will be a classic "Type A" personality. Possibly even a workaholic, driven to correct every detail of any project they begin.

Other types might let go and relax when the work is pretty well finished, but Ones aren't so easy on themselves. They need to make sure everything is done right. And they may very well resent others who don't try as hard as they (constantly) try to live up to high standards.

Not surprisingly, anger is the fatal flaw of a One. It's a logical response when someone lets down the team, and people with strong beliefs in right and wrong will frequently see that happen. Yet because anger may not always be a socially acceptable response, Ones will often try to stuff it down and ignore it.

Along those same lines, they'll deny their own desire for anything that might not be considered good, right and true. Ones are rarely overweight, because they're able to resist the lure of hot fudge sundaes better than most types.

They're used to ignoring their own "incorrect" preferences in favor of what's correct, controlling not just the world around them but their own emotions as well. And if that means denying any sense of anger, they'll do it.

So you can imagine a character whose high standards have slipped for just a moment, horrified at such a lapse. In the face of anger, the One can either feel guilty – or shift the blame outward.

The idea that Everyone Deserves A Second Chance is foreign to a One…and as this character approaches a happy ending, that can be a powerful realization. "Even if I made a mistake, I can still be a fundamentally decent person." Most types recognize that with no problem, but for a One it's a dramatic turnaround.

Ones As Children

Even as children, Ones are concerned with doing the right thing. They're a stern, stuffy grandparent's pride and joy, because they'll master the fundamentals of showing respect and using the right fork and tying shoelaces neatly at a very young age. Their focus is on living up to expectations, no matter what those expectations may be.

So if a One is raised by parents who preach nontraditional informality, that will become as rigid a standard of behavior as the conventional good manners of a One raised by traditional parents. Either way, the child is likely to notice that nobody else seems to worry quite as much about upholding the rules…and conclude that it's a struggle better kept private.

But the struggle will continue, as the little One tries to avoid doing anything that can't be done perfectly. Compromise is not an option. In fact, the One might even take on the role of a parent, supervising everyone in the household, with an emphasis on either moral or physical cleanliness.

Whether the One believes in ethical behavior or keeping the room free of dust, there's always a yearning for recognition. A blue ribbon or a pat on the back means more than this child will ever reveal, because "wanting praise would be greedy." But that blue ribbon will be treasured for years.

The lucky Ones are those whose parents encourage them to explore what they truly want, not just what they *should* want. But no matter what they value deep inside, they'll continue trying to make the world a better place…through hard work and a strong sense of personal responsibility. "If *I* don't save the world," an earnest young One might explain, "who will?"

Ones At Work

Whether as a boss or an employee, Ones like having specific timetables and guidelines. They like being accountable for what they do, and they like everyone else to be accountable as well.

Which makes sense, considering that they're conscientious about taking responsibility for their own performance. Give them a good cause to work for, and they'll work as hard as it takes. The only thing they'll have a hard time with is delegating…because who knows if someone else will take the job as seriously as they do?

Ones are not only good with details – some might say overly concerned with details – but they're also tremendously disciplined, honest and ethical. They won't hesitate to uphold every professional standard laid down by the hierarchy, because they respect the rules of an organization.

If they have to work late because an order was delayed by the weather, they'll do it with good cheer. If they have to work late because an order was delayed by carelessness, they'll be furious.

But when they identify with the goal of a team or workplace, they'll support it with everything they've got. They'll put their logical, analytical skills to work. They'll put their grit and determination straight to work. They'll even persuade others to work, by exemplifying such passionate commitment that people can't help jumping on board.

Ones are known among their co-workers for doing a good job, and by their employees for maintaining consistent fairness and balance. What they want to avoid is being wrong…and if that means turning down new opportunities that involve some risk, or shifting blame when something doesn't turn out right, they might consider such options. What matters most is improving the world around them, and Ones will do whatever it takes to make that happen.

Ones In Relationships

Ones want things to be fair. Fair is good. Fair is right. So they'll go out of their way to make sure they treat everyone fairly – if you had dinner on *their* side of town last time, they'll make sure that next time it's on your side.

They want to be appreciated by everyone around them, and they make a point of appreciating the best in others as well. They want to do their part for the relationship, and they expect others to do the same.

They're tremendously loyal to the people they love, and they expect loyalty in return. Fair is fair.

But with their black-and-white view of the world, Ones can get very confused if they ever wind up feeling angry with people they love. "How can I be upset about Devon canceling lunch, when

I love Devon more than anyone in the world?" It takes a lot of insight for Ones to grasp that not every relationship is black-and-white, that you can feel more than one emotion for the same person.

And the people who truly care about Ones may need to remind them that mistakes are part of life, that anger doesn't negate love, and that forgiveness is always possible.

Ones have a hard time forgiving themselves for errors. If they fiercely disapprove of some trait in a friend – say, lateness – it's a safe bet that lateness is something they struggle with themselves.

Any relationship they're in, they'll want to improve. Sure, that means expecting the best of their loved ones. But they expect the same thing of themselves. Ones who see any opportunity for making a relationship better – even if it means overlooking a few flaws – will do whatever they can to be the best possible partner, lover and friend.

One's Individual Subtype

Ones whose subtype is self-preservation tend to worry. Endlessly. Especially about the tools for survival, which for most people translates into material wealth.

Worry might become a type of magic for them. "I worried all last year about the furnace breaking down and it didn't break down, so clearly the way to keep the furnace going is to worry about it."

They might focus all their concern on details like the furnace to avoid worrying about anything larger, such as what they want out of life. "I can't think about that right now; I'm too concerned with that knock in the engine."

Since safety is a primary concern, they'll extend it to their loved ones as well. These Ones may be overly nurturing, overly critical, or both. Whatever it takes to keep Junior safe, they'll do. And if they perceive life as coming down to a choice between safety and happiness, safety will win every time.

In a world which requires their constant vigilance to keep from collapsing, it's only natural that these self-preservation Ones will be afraid of making mistakes. If avoiding a project altogether will ensure that they can't possibly make a mistake, they'll become champion procrastinators.

But any neighborhood watch group with a One like this on the team will never have to worry about being caught off guard. When One is on the job, all's right with the world.

One's Intimacy Subtype

Ones who put intimate relationships at the top of their priority list will be the type to carry their loved one's photo at all times. They'll speak of them with deep respect.

They'll live with high ideals for not only the relationship, but also for themselves individually, and of course they'll want their partner to uphold those same ideals.

Their quest for perfection might be rooted partly in the fear of abandonment. "If I'm not the best person I can be at all times, how can I expect anyone to keep loving me?"

When they *do* find someone who seems to love them even in spite of occasional failures, they're astonished. And relieved. And worried. What if they mess things up? What if someone more attractive steals this perfect person away?

Jealousy comes easily to a One whose partner seems perfect – and the partner *has* to be perfect, because otherwise why would the One be interested?

It may be tempting to criticize flaws in a friend or mate, because the One can't help but seeing how very close this person is to sheer perfection. If only it weren't for that annoying little habit of humming off-key....

That's the only down side of being idealized by a One. Which makes it important to remind your loving One that mistakes are okay, even forgivable. And that the relationship matters to you both, so you might as well relax and enjoy it.

One's Social Subtype

Ones who value "the entire group" will naturally seek out societies whose values mirror their own. It makes sense to spend time with friends who share their beliefs, rather than with strangers who don't.

Coming from a position of strength means belonging to a group where everyone agrees on the same rules. Because rules are important. Rules keep things orderly.

Social-subtype Ones feel better when they're part of a larger social order or a longstanding tradition – whether it's religious, political, corporate, scholastic or anything else – where the rules apply to all people at all times. Sure, that might seem kind of inflexible, but it's a small price to pay for belonging to such a terrific group.

Information which contradicts their beliefs is hard to assimilate, and these Ones know how to deal with such a threat. They dismiss it. "Maybe I don't quite understand how X can be true and Y can also be true, but if that's what our leader says then I'm sure it's correct."

Regardless of how strongly they identify with their chosen society, though, Ones won't hesitate to speak up if they see something that deviates from their own principles. Because no matter how much they value the traditions and rules and morals of their own beloved group, at heart they still believe in making things right for the world…no matter what it takes to accomplish that.

Ones With Other Types

Ones are great at doing what's right, but that doesn't provide much conflict for an author. Instead, take a look at what can go wrong when a One encounters any of the nine types.

One & One

Both believe in upholding the highest standards. But if their standards differ, there'll be fireworks. Each is convinced that *this* way is right, so *that* way is wrong, and compromise means giving up what's correct for what's flawed. Not a possibility.

One & Two

One knows things will be fine if everyone does their part. Two wants to make sure everyone's happy. "Personal feelings aren't as important as the overall concept," says One. "Personal feelings are more important than *any* concept!"

One & Three

One wants to get this done right no matter how long it takes; Three wants to get it done in a blaze of glory by Friday. Three leaps into action, and One pulls back. Each feels impatient and frustrated: "Doesn't this person *get* it?"

One & Four

One wants to control emotions; Four wants to express them. "But I'm just so upset!" "Come on, get hold of yourself. I'm upset, too, but you don't see me getting all whacked out." "You've never been in touch with your feelings."

One & Five

Five wants to focus on the new research; One wants to focus on getting the current job done *right* – too bad if that means interrupting Five. Five shuts the door. One takes offense. Five opens it and sighs. One blows up.

One & Six

One's upset about something, but doesn't like to gripe. Six is aware of One fuming, and starts to worry. "Did I do something wrong?" "No, everything's fine." "But you're clenching your teeth." "I am *not!*" "Uh-oh, what did I *do?*"

One & Seven

One wants to make sure all the details are taken care of. Seven wants to let all the details take care of themselves. "Look, if you'd just take some responsibility once in a while..." "Look, if you'd just lighten up once in a while..."

One & Eight

Both have strong feelings, but One cares more about public opinion than Eight. "Knock it off, One, you're too judgmental." "Well, if you'd look at yourself you'd see I'm right." "You *always* think you're right." "I always am."

One & Nine

One has a plan for Tuesday, while Nine just wants to relax. "Relaxing is fine in its place, but we need to get things straightened out." "You can handle it without me." "But that's not fair." Nine shrugs. One fumes. Nine retreats...

You see how none of these is a life-and-death conflict? But each one can be intensified or relieved, depending on where you are in the story.

Some conflicts may strike you as overly dramatic or overly boring. That's okay. That's a clear sign that your story doesn't *need* such a conflict. You may have enough conflict already. If you do need more, though, it's a safe bet that at least one of these examples will spark some ideas. And that's where the fun begins.

Scenarios With Ones

No matter what kind of story you're telling, the characters' personality types will make a difference in the conflict that arises. Here are examples of five stories – about a detective, a princess, a cowboy, a teenager and a career woman – where the protagonist will come into conflict because of his or her enneagram type.

= = = = = = = =

Let's start with the cop trying to track down a blackmailer who's threatening the arrogant father-in-law of his beloved daughter. Jack Warner is a One, which explains why he became a cop in the first place. He believes in law and order, and he's going to do his best to make sure the laws are followed and the city is safe.

Even though he doesn't much like Karen's father-in-law, he knows that blackmail is a crime and that fighting crime is his job. Besides, disliking Karen's father-in-law is petty behavior. Not what he expects of himself.

So what if the guy is arrogant? So what if he thinks *he* knows all the answers? Jack's not going to let that keep him from doing the best possible job.

But it annoys him when the guy doesn't even show up on time for their meeting to discuss the letters. Okay, yeah, he's being judgmental. Gotta stop that. Gotta focus on the job.

Jack's good at his job. He's earned commendations from the top brass, leaders who evidently recognize – along with his fellow officers – that here's somebody who will never, ever go against procedure. Who'll follow every rule in the book. Who'll never look the other way at any infraction, even if it means giving up his holiday to prosecute minor criminals another cop would simply let go.

Jack's not built that way. He doesn't cut corners, he doesn't take shortcuts, and he doesn't give up on making the world a better place.

Which means doing his best to catch this blackmailer. It's just so damned annoying – oops, gotta watch the language, there might be children in the precinct office. It's just so *darned* annoying that Karen's father-in-law doesn't seem to realize what a tough job this is. If they've set their meeting for two o'clock, what gives him the right to show up at two-thirty?

Jack's almost tempted to show up late himself, but that's not the kind of behavior he can justify. What's the matter with him, anyway, getting upset over something this insignificant? He's a cop, he stands for truth and justice, and getting angry about stupid little things is unacceptable.

But when the guy finally strolls in at three o'clock without so much as an apology, Jack blows up. "If it weren't for my daughter,

I wouldn't give you the time of day!" Now he's even more upset. How could he lose control like that, especially in front of Karen's father-in-law? Why can't he keep a lid on his emotions? He's got to make things better. He's got to make things right....

= = = = = = = =

Next comes the princess trying to choose the best ally to defend her kingdom from an invasion of trolls – either the renegade dragon-rider, or the vampire lord.

As a One, Aliana is used to making tough decisions. It's for the good of the kingdom, and she's never been the type to shirk her responsibilities. But this looks like an especially difficult choice, because she really can't bring herself to approve of an alliance with someone like Kelwyn – who's just too disorganized when it comes to tracking dragons – or with someone like Varek – who has this bizarre taste for human blood.

If only there were some neighbor whose standards she could approve of! Life would certainly be simpler if she could forget about these pesky notions of right and wrong, which don't seem to trouble any of her courtiers or handmaidens.

Still, she has to do what's right. And if that means swallowing her distaste for the dragon-rider or the vampire lord in order to save the kingdom, she'll do the best job she possibly can.

Probably the best way to choose, Aliana decides, is to hold a banquet. Invite them both. See who seems closer to her own ideal of the perfect ally.

She can't help feeling a stir of wistfulness when she sees Varek glide in without even bothering to kiss her jewel-studded scepter – imagine disregarding propriety to that degree! – and a pang of envy when she sees Kelwyn quaff two deep goblets of wine without any thought for how it might affect him come morning. Imagine living solely for the moment, the way this dragon-rider does.

But of course she doesn't want that kind of life for herself. Absolutely not. Dreaming of freedom is silly, wasteful, a denial of everything she believes in. No, what matters is doing her duty. And her duty tonight is to choose an ally, not to sit around wishing her life were different.

Still, the image of Kelwyn's carefree attitude lingers with her, and she decides to choose him. Her handmaiden observes with a wink that it's easy to see why Aliana made that choice – "I saw the way you were looking at him" – and Aliana feels a flash of anger. Which of course she can't show, because a princess doesn't flare up at commoners. Instead she says coolly that it's for the good of the kingdom, but inside she's shaken. Could she really have put her personal feelings ahead of her responsibilities?

Maybe she'll deny any mistake. Maybe she'll rush to correct it but dread making another, which makes her stumble again. Maybe she'll learn to forgive herself…but when?

= = = = = = = =

Now, here's our cowboy facing off against the cattle rustlers. Buck is a One, and he knows he can't let those dratted rustlers get away with breaking the law like that. Not only are they robbing the Triple C, but they're acting like they have every right to take what they want and hang the consequences.

That isn't the kind of business any right-thinking man can put up with. No, he'll have to teach those rustlers a thing or two.

Buck formulates a plan to catch 'em in the act, but it'll require the help of the foreman at the Triple D and another couple of cowboys from the Triple E. No problem, he'll go explain how things need to be done. Then they can line up their men, nab the rustlers and hand 'em over to the sheriff once and for all.

Except the Triple D foreman has a whole different idea about how to handle the rustlers. Buck knows he can't just call the fellow a stupid coward, but how on earth could anyone believe such a stupid, cowardly plan would work? Does this blasted foreman really think they can talk sense into the rustlers at the town picnic, when clearly it makes more sense to trap them for the sheriff? It's a wonder the Triple D is even still around, with a foreman who thinks like that.

But things don't go any better with those cowboys from the Triple E. They've got some crazy notion that the simplest way to fix this trouble is to lie in wait and shoot the rustlers in the back. What kind of hare-brained scheme is that? How can any man call himself a cowboy if he doesn't have the guts to square off against an enemy face to face? Haven't these fellows ever heard of a little thing called honor?

No, the only way to handle this is by following the plan Buck has come up with. Right is right, after all, and the Triple D and Triple E guys will have to acknowledge that. You can't be lily-livered and survive out West. You can't be sneaky and take any pride in your name. Why can't he make them understand that?

Even worse, they're all trying to change *his* mind about what's right and what's wrong. Here he's trying to make the world a better place, and what kind of thanks is he getting? People who can't even appreciate the best way to get things done are calling *him* stubborn, and Buck's getting fed up. If he has to tame the West all by himself, well, then, that's just what he's gonna do.

= = = = = = = =

Let's take a look at the teenager whose only friend finds a buried treasure in the family's backyard.

Jamie is a One, which means that deciding what to do with buried treasure is no challenge at all. It clearly belongs to whoever buried it there, unless of course the treasure was stolen, in which case it belongs to the rightful owner. Case closed. It's that simple.

But Kelly doesn't seem to see things in such black-and-white terms, which is a little baffling. A little troubling, as well, because they've been friends for quite a while – seems like a lot of the kids in school think Jamie is too straight to be much fun – and it's disturbing that Kelly doesn't grasp the fundamental difference between right and wrong. Kelly's got this idea that the treasure belongs to whoever found it, and that makes things difficult.

Jamie can't exactly turn in half the treasure and pretend the other half never turned up. That might sound easier, but it'd be tough to get away with a story like that – cousin T.J. has always warned that "you'll never make it as a poker player," which Jamie suspects is true. Lying would be handy, but it's not really an option. So it looks like there's a dilemma, here. Is it better to do the right thing in terms of what's legal, or is better to do the right thing in terms of supporting a friend?

Maybe it'd be different if Kelly didn't need the money. But with a sick baby in the family and a dad who lost his job three months ago, there's no use pretending things aren't tough over there. Still, what about the rightful owner? What if they need the money just as much?

Jamie doesn't know where to turn. Normally there are pretty clear rules about right and wrong, a code of ethics that makes it easy to figure out what to do.

Not like it's always easy, doing the right thing, but nobody ever said life was easy. On the other hand, nobody ever anticipated a situation like this.

What's really aggravating is that Kelly doesn't seem to understand how tricky this is. Jamie's torn between what's legally right and what's morally right, and here Kelly's trying to make it into a simple question of "stick by your friends." But what if that's not the right thing to do? And how can Kelly act like it's no big deal?

A lot of possibilities for growth, here. A lot of ways to make things even worse, and to offer a triumphant conclusion. What'll work best for your story?

= = = = = = = =

Finally, the career woman who hires a detective to find the baby she gave up for adoption 13 years ago. As a One, Anne might have had any number of reasons for the adoption – let's say she knew the right thing to do was to give this baby a family that could offer the loving support every child deserves.

But now she's discovered some rare disease which the adoptive parents must be warned about, and she's determined to do the right thing. So she hires a detective to locate her daughter, and though he offers to break the news himself, Anne won't evade a tough job. She insists on being kept in the loop, so she can determine the best way to approach Emily's parents. She's going to do this correctly.

What she hasn't planned on is her unexpected attraction to the detective. She can't let herself give into such feelings, not in the middle of a search. She has to keep her priorities straight, and distracting Craig from his work would be flat-out wrong.

Yet he seems just as intrigued by her. He even coaxes her into taking an hour off from her dogged internet-searching by insisting that she'll work better after a relaxing dinner. Something about this man makes her wish she could give into the desire for an easier life, for an afternoon of fun here and there, for –

No. No, she can't think that way. Not when she has a warning to deliver. What's she doing, putting her own wishes ahead of the greater good? She knows better than that!

Anne redoubles her efforts to concentrate on the job, but Craig isn't making it easy. He seems to think she should give herself a break every now and then, not beat up on herself for every little mistake – but he doesn't understand how important it is to stay on the right track. He believes in appreciating the beauty of a sunset, the pleasure of music, the peace of a starry night, and that might be fine except she has goals to fulfill. She can't just relax her standards and forget her responsibilities. She did that back in high school, the night of the junior prom, and look how *that* turned out.

Suppose they find Emily and it turns out she's a lot like Anne. Very concerned with doing what's right, very reluctant to forgive herself for doing anything wrong. Will that make Anne realize that

Craig's right about the importance of letting go? Or make her all the more determined to set a good example?

But would atoning for old sins make Emily feel like a mistake? What's she going to do?

Keep in mind that even if she learns to forgive honest mistakes, she's still a One. A happier, healthier One who's overcome the fatal flaw of anger – cracking down on anyone who violates the rules, especially herself – but a One nonetheless.

Nobody changes their type. They can change their outlook on life, they can change the traits which have kept them from being the best they can be, but their fundamental type never changes.

Because remember how all nine types can be terrific people? A happy ending just means that this particular type has found their best self. A tragic ending means they've found it and turned away. An either-way ending means they haven't found it yet...but maybe they will in the next story.

You're the writer. You can pick. And readers who share your view of the world will be delighted with whatever choice you make.

CHAPTER TWO

QUIZ

- ☐ Do you like to be needed?
- ☐ Do you try hard to be thoughtful and tactful?
- ☐ Do you feel irritated when people break rules?
- ☐ Do you enjoy giving people compliments?
- ☐ Would you rather give than receive?
- ☐ Do people find you enthusiastic and upbeat?
- ☐ Do people seek you out to talk about their problems?
- ☐ Do most people like you?
- ☐ Do you enjoy helping others become more successful?
- ☐ Do you often feel taken for granted?

___ **TOTAL FOR TWO**

TYPE TWO: The Giver, The Helper, The Nurturer

If you've ever met someone who seemed to know instinctively what you needed – and who was always ready to provide advice, assistance and encouragement at a moment's notice – you've met the best possible Two.

If that same person started nagging you about not appreciating such devoted support, complaining that nobody understands how much *work* it takes to be a constant fountain of love, you've met a less stellar Two.

Either way, you get the picture. Twos love to give. They love to help. They love to provide whatever people around them need, whether it's emotional nurturance or physical maintenance, a well-planned celebration or a spontaneous gift. They want to help you become the best you can be, and they'll throw themselves wholeheartedly into the job of protecting your best interests.

Sometimes the loved one winds up feeling smothered or manipulated. But when the Two is truly giving just for the sake of giving, the loved one feels bathed in altruistic compassion, empathy and support.

Twos identify with other people's needs. It's easy for them to see what will please those around them. And because they feel best about themselves when they're giving to others, they work doggedly to provide others with genuine caring, attention and unconditional love.

You see this all the time in new parents, whose entire lives are centered on creating a perfect environment for the world's most wonderful baby. New lovers, too, will frequently show that same rapturous attention to granting every possible wish their darling might express. Someone with a family member suffering some serious illness will devote long hours to offering comfort and help.

But once the patient has recovered, the lovers have settled into a comfortable routine, or the baby is starting to walk and talk, most people stop spending every moment working to fulfill their loved one's most cherished dreams.

Except for Twos.

Their entire well-being is wrapped up in caring for others. They often don't recognize any needs of their own, like the noble stereotype of a character who will starve to death rather than take a crust of bread from a mildly hungry friend.

Of course, the best adjusted Twos will *share* the bread, realizing that everyone – including themselves – deserves enough to eat. But no Two will ever grab the entire loaf and run off to devour it alone, because helping other people is built into Two's very soul.

Living alone on a desert island would be sheer misery for Twos. There's nobody to look out for, nobody to take care of, nobody to prove they're needed. They may come to depend on feeling essential, fearing they won't be loved unless they earn it through constant service.

Fortunately, most Twos don't have to live alone. They can always find people who need help, and they're extremely good at determining what someone needs.

If one friend needs to be cheered up, they'll put on a clown suit. If a neighbor needs help filling out forms, they'll put on a pair of glasses. If Mom needs fashion advice, they'll put on comfortable shoes and drag her off to the mall.

It might appear that the Two is simply playing a series of roles, from clown to tax advisor to shopping escort all within a few hours, but in fact each role is a genuine part of this person. Twos are gifted with adaptability, although they can wear themselves out meeting the needs of too many different people. But since meeting others' needs provides them with the sustenance *they* need, they'll keep at it long after another type might stop and say, "Wait, I've gotta have time for myself!"

Twos rarely take time for themselves. Sure, they might feel confined by the demands of so many people clamoring for support, but what better way to *know* they're needed? What better way to keep others happy? What better way to live?

Famous Twos

Probably the most famous example of Two's innately nurturing style would be Jesus Christ, who embodied the essence of caring for others with no thought for personal reward. Mother Teresa is another example of non-stop service, not for fame or recognition – after all, she labored for years before attracting attention from the world – but simply for the joy of helping those in need.

Compared to those Twos, others might seem a little more worldly. But since people who spend their lives working quietly to help others rarely draw great public acclaim, that's no surprise.

Even so, you can see the Two attitude toward improving life for others in people like Princess Diana, who used her fame to raise money for children. Mahatma Ghandi, who took it upon himself to make things better for the people of India. Florence Nightingale, who left the comforts of a wealthy family to struggle in the Crimea, carrying that famous lamp to soldiers' bedsides night after endless night.

Twos might turn their nurturing attention more to just one person than to the entire world, and we see that in people like Nancy Reagan and Yoko Ono. Or they might work for the good of people they'll never meet, like Jerry Lewis with his fund-raising for muscular dystrophy…Betty Friedan with her campaigns for women's rights…and Mr. Rogers, who gave children a place where they could feel good about themselves just by turning on the TV.

It's even visible in celebrities who show more genuine warmth than we expect from celebrities – like Bill Cosby, Alan Alda and Laura Bush. Anyone who makes you feel better just by saying hello is more than likely a Two.

Two's Heroic Strengths

Just as you'd expect from people who like to make you feel good, Twos never hesitate to offer a hello or a hug. They don't hold back from expressing affection, although if they know you're embarrassed by a public display they'll be extremely discreet.

They don't give love to get love – they give it because love is meant to be shared. They truly want the best for you, and it has nothing to do with whether your success will make them look good. If you have the skill to become a great soccer player, they'll support you all the way. But if you decide soccer isn't your choice after all, they'll never prod you to reconsider.

These Twos are willing to let people be themselves. At the same time, though, they see the best in everyone and have a way of sensing what will make you happy…then offering steady, cheerful encouragement no matter how tough the road to happiness might be. And if your road leads you to the other side of the world, they won't hold you back. They'll pack you a lunch and wave you off with a fond farewell.

Doing good is important to Twos, but they don't care who gets the credit for it. What matters is that people get what they need.

Healthy Twos are remarkably humble – especially when you consider how much they have to be proud of – but for them the whole point of service is to make things better. It's not about their own ego. It's about the good of mankind.

So the best Twos in your life will be generous, charitable, thoughtful and encouraging. Well-meaning, warmhearted, nurturing and sincere. They'll empower you to discover your strengths and cheer every success. What's not to love about a Two?

Two's Fatal Flaws

What's not to love? Well, a Two *can* be overbearing. If you've ever heard someone say, "I know what's best for you, so listen up," you're seeing the bossy side of a Two.

Because they find their identity in helping others, they can become wrapped up in feeling essential. Their fatal flaw, then, is pride. Pride in being the person everyone depends on, pride in being indispensable. A Two might deny any such thing, insisting that "I only look out for John and Betsy – and Kathy, Ken, Derek, Monica, Heather, Joan and Sinclair – because they can't look out for themselves," but there's a certain amount of pride involved in such a claim.

It's only natural that Twos who feel worthless unless they're needed will be deeply hurt if their sacrifices aren't acknowledged.

They want recognition and appreciation for everything they've done to help, and that adds up to a lot. Maybe their help is exactly what you needed, or possibly it's only what they *thought* you needed, but either way they want some acknowledgment.

Which makes sense. If the only way a Two can feel worthwhile is from feeling needed, of course they'll do whatever they can to be needed. They'll flatter, seduce and manipulate. They'll be possessive, intrusive and martyr-like. But they'll do it all while insisting that it's not the least bit selfish; it's all about "making sure other people get what *they* need. I don't *have* any needs of my own!"

They may never stop to consider their own preferences, having spent their lives focused on others. But once they *do* acknowledge that of course they have needs and wants of their own, Twos will begin to nurture from the strength of love rather than from the weakness of pride...and that's where the happy ending begins.

Twos As Children

Love is important to little Twos, and they'll do their best to earn it by whatever means will draw the most approval from their parents and teachers and friends. If making straight A's wins a pat on the back, they'll study all night long. If listening to someone's problems earns a heartfelt thanks, they'll spend hours on the phone. If looking tidy generates goodwill, they'll be the neatest-looking children in town.

The only time they might stop looking perfect is if a lost dog is trapped in the mud. An immediate need for help will always win out over the prospect of approval a few hours from now, so any Two who sees the opportunity to provide assistance won't hesitate to offer it. Too bad if their best clothes got muddy, the dog *needed* to be rescued!

Like their adult counterparts, young Twos are good at reading people. They know what each friend and each parent and each neighbor likes best, and they'll adapt their personality to meet the needs of whomever they're with.

Of course, that can be tough if they're in a Scout troop where each friend likes a different aspect of their personality. It's easy to get worn out facing so many demands, and the lucky little Twos are those whose parents ensure that they get plenty of time to explore their own interests.

Which might take some effort, because Twos don't naturally seek out the opportunity to be alone. Not when there are so many opportunities to be with friends who can offer the approval they yearn for.

But taking time to focus on what *they* want, even when it's in the company of a friend, will help them realize that meeting others' needs isn't the only road to self-esteem.

Twos At Work

Clients and customers love Twos. Who else would devote such thoughtful attention to making sure their every need is met? Twos in any workplace that emphasizes personal service are in their element, able to use their astonishing skills of empathy and understanding to make everyone's day go better.

They like being acknowledged for their service, as well, although if there's a monthly prize for Most Thoughtful Employee and they know Jan wants to win it just as much as they do, they'll find themselves in a terrible bind. Which matters more, winning acclaim or making Jan happy?

Often they settle into a position of being the power behind the throne, focusing all their attention on a boss who gets the public acclaim and taking satisfaction in knowing it would never happen without their support.

Because they're so good at reading people, a Two can tell you every detail about everyone on the job. They know who likes whom, who'd rather not work around whom, and they're always up to date on the latest developments. If there's an "in" group and an "out" group, you can guess where you're most likely to find the Two.

No matter what the job, Two wants some emotional connection to it. Maybe "this paycheck enables me to support my loved ones," or maybe "this project will make life better for everyone who lives near First & Main."

If they're in charge of a project, they'll surround themselves with people who share their vision of success built with loving care. And if they're in charge of choosing people, their selections will be based more on individual personality than on black-and-white credentials. After all, what matters most is how people feel about the job, and about themselves.

Twos In Relationships

Because they care so deeply about the opinions of people around them, Twos are especially vulnerable to the threat of rejection. They tend to compensate for that by becoming indispensable, by doing whatever it takes to make sure people continue relying on their help and support.

This means they might become so focused on pleasing their friends or partners that they completely ignore their own feelings. "Me? I'm fine, I have everything I want. As long as *you're* happy." So if you're in a relationship with a Two, the best thing you can do is to encourage exploration of individual needs. "What I want is to give *you* a treat. What's your favorite food?"

Letting go of their usual I'm-only-here-to-help-you position can be scary for Twos. They're used to giving, not receiving. And they might deliberately steer clear of relationships where it looks like both parties will be equal, where there's a strong possibility of genuine intimacy.

That way there's no worry about being rejected by someone who truly knows them for who they are.

Of course, it can be very tempting to just sit back and enjoy Two's flattering attention. But there's always the risk that the Two will eventually get tired of peeling another grape and demand some reward for all that faithful service. If the reward doesn't arrive, they might finally storm off in a huff and tell you to meet your own needs for a change.

It's far better to reassure the Two, right from the start, that love doesn't have to be earned...and that while you appreciate having your fruit peeled, you'll love them even if they simply hand you a banana and let you peel it yourself.

Two's Individual Subtype

For an individual-subtype Two, self-preservation is all about entitlement. And who's more entitled to rewards than someone who devotes every waking minute to the service of others?

This subtype Two *expects* acknowledgment. Preferential treatment. Applause, support, recognition...you name it and they deserve it.

If they throw a fabulous dinner party for twelve and get only eleven thank-you notes, they'll feel downright slighted. Maybe it was obvious that the twelfth guest had a wonderful time, but not sending a note is inexcusable! Doesn't anyone understand the importance of acknowledgment?

So, feeling entitled to special recognition and acknowledgment, the Two will take whatever steps necessary to ensure it's forthcoming.

They might seek out people to pamper and assist, who in turn will provide *them* with financial or emotional support. They might reward themselves for being such great nurturers by arranging glorious vacations, or exceptional foods in the pantry, or shopping trips that wind up costing more than their budget allows – but considering how much they do for others, aren't they entitled to spend a little more?

Indulging themselves allows them to return their attention to others, providing all the helpful strength they're used to giving.

If they feel the least bit needy, they immediately bury that need by doing something for someone else. With any luck, they'll choose someone whose success will reflect well on them – because that way they can enjoy the fruits of triumph without ever having to risk any failure of their own.

Two's Intimacy Subtype

For a Two who likes intimate relationships, there are always new friends to be made. Whether the connection is romantic or just friendly, they're gifted at making people want to be with them. They know how to listen attentively, how to exude just the right level of smoldering sexuality, how to remember favorite drinks and movies and activities in order to entice all the love and attraction they want.

They enjoy being someone's favorite companion, a treasured confidante. They'll pursue as many people as they can, in order to assure themselves of having someone to call whenever they want company.

Being alone, being ignored is intolerable, and they'll do whatever they can to avoid being overlooked. If that means going after every new friend they can possibly meet, so be it.

Being wanted by other people makes these Twos feel valued and loved, and they'll do whatever it takes to be wanted. They might not want the actual intimacy that comes with a longtime mate, but they know how to avoid that. Just go after people who are unavailable. The thrill of the chase can be enough, especially for a Two who knows how easy it is to lose oneself in a long-term commitment.

Better to keep things open-ended. Better not to settle down with just one person who might someday walk out. Better to keep lots and lots and lots of people happy.

Two's Social Subtype

When a Two puts the social group ahead of everything else, there are a number of routes to take.

One might be the "stage mother," throwing every ounce of energy into grooming someone else for public acclaim.

Another might be the "right-hand man," providing such great backup for a successful leader that it'd be hard to imagine doing without this devoted Two.

Another might be the "hub of the family," staying in touch with everyone and relaying news and hosting holiday dinners to the point where everyone relies on the loyal Two to keep the family together.

Society-minded Twos hate to be left out, so they'll work at becoming irreplaceable. They might affiliate with someone who shows strong potential for winning success and acclaim, because that's a sure way of guaranteeing arrival at the top.

And the top is a great place to be, since these Twos adore public recognition for their work. Which might leave them frustrated when they watch someone they've supported now reaping all the glory.

Being noticed, they believe, is the same as being loved. And being ignored is such a horrible prospect that they'd rather make a scene than be overlooked.

Still, as long as they can be valued for their warmth, friendliness, energy or expertise, the social-subtype Twos are perfectly happy. Give them a chance to make a difference in people's lives, and they'll meet the challenge with flying colors.

Twos With Other Types

Twos are great at helping friends and nurturing loved ones, but that doesn't provide much conflict for an author. Instead, take a look at what can go wrong when a Two encounters any of the nine types.

Two & One

Two wants to make sure everyone's happy; One knows things will be fine if everyone does their part. "Personal feelings aren't as important as the overall concept," says One. "Personal feelings are more important than *any* concept!"

Two & Two

"We'll do whatever you want to do." "No, we'll do whatever you want to do." "You decide; I want to make you happy." "You do too much for me as it is; I want you to decide." "It'll make me happy if you go first." "No, you go first."

Two & Three

Two wants to offer support during Three's big project; Three is too busy for support right now. "I'm fine, go take care of someone else." "But I'm here for *you!*" "I've got to get this done." "You won't let yourself need anyone."

Two & Four

Four is feeling melancholy, so Two offers a kindly pat on the back. "There, there, I'll make you some tea." "Tea won't help, I need to mourn." "But I want you to feel better." "Can't you just let me grieve?" "I don't understand." "You sure don't."

Two & Five

Two sees Five wrapped up in solitude and asks, "Would you like a sandwich?" "No, I'm busy." "But you need nourishment." "No, thanks." "But I want to take care of you." "I don't need it!" "What, you don't need *me*?"

Two & Six

Since Six is always analyzing motives, Two's usual style of nurturing might arouse some suspicion. "You're not buttering my toast because you care about me; it's only so I'll need you." "I'm just trying to be helpful." "No, there's more to it than that."

Two & Seven

Here's where the desire to nurture meets the desire for freedom. "I just want to know where we stand," says Two. "You're obsessing about our relationship," says Seven. "Can't you give me some clue?" "Can't you give me some *space*?"

Two & Eight

"Oh, dear," sighs Two, "you hurt someone's feelings at the party." "Come on, I was just being myself," protests Eight. "You know how much I love you, so why do you always make things hard for me?" "Why do you always sigh at me?"

Two & Nine

Two wants to talk about a problem between them. Nine would rather withdraw. Two cries, "I need interaction." Nine retreats to the bedroom and shuts the door. Two feels neglected and ignored. Nine feels invaded and pursued.

You see how none of these is a life-and-death conflict? But each one can be intensified or relieved, depending on where you are in the story.

Some conflicts may strike you as overly dramatic or overly boring. That's okay. That's a clear sign that your story doesn't *need* such a conflict. You may have enough conflict already. If you do need more, though, it's a safe bet that at least one of these examples will spark some ideas. And that's where the fun begins.

Scenarios With Twos

No matter what kind of story you're telling, the characters' personality types will make a difference in the conflict that arises. Here are examples of five stories – about a detective, a princess, a cowboy, a teenager and a career woman – where the protagonist will come into conflict because of his or her enneagram type.

= = = = = = = = =

Let's start with the cop trying to track down a blackmailer who's threatening the arrogant father-in-law of his beloved daughter. Jack Warner is a Two, so helping Karen is right at the top of his list. Even if he doesn't much like her father-in-law, he'll do whatever he can for his precious daughter.

After all, Karen deserves whatever he can give her. So does her mom, and he's spent a lifetime providing Mary and Karen with all the loving attention and gifts he can manage.

Sometimes it annoys him that they don't seem to realize how much he actually *does* for them, but Jack dismisses that thought as selfish. Nobody can ever accuse Jack Warner of being selfish.

Not his family, and not the police department. He gives a hundred and ten percent to the job, at least during the workday, and a hundred and twenty percent to his wife. Now that their daughter has gotten married and left home, he has more free time to help Mary organize her quilting projects, deal with the landscaping crew, and plan fun evenings for the neighbors. Mary deserves all the help he can give her, and their parties are always a special event.

Jack's proud of that – or he would be, if he were the kind of guy who went around feeling proud.

But of course he can't really take pride in doing what comes naturally, in making sure that everyone at the party has a great time. That's just the way he is. After all, what fun would it be if someone else was miserable?

Right now, though, Karen's father-in-law is miserable. Even though the guy is too cocky to admit it, Jack's good at reading people's feelings, and he knows this blackmail threat is painful. So if he can make things better for everyone, there's no question that he'll do whatever he can.

Maybe it means working extra hours, which wouldn't bother him except that it means leaving Mary alone. He hates to do that, because Mary *needs* him. She might say she's perfectly content having the house to herself, but Jack knows that isn't true. Without him there to look out for her, Mary would be lonely in no time.

But she insists that helping Karen's in-laws is more important, so Jack decides he'll make it up to her later and concentrate on the job. There's something inherently satisfying about police work, knowing he's helping people who need his skill. Even if they never acknowledge it, which they rarely do, this time will surely be the exception. His daughter and the in-laws will be tremendously grateful. Jack can see it now…

= = = = = = = =

Next comes the princess trying to choose the best ally to defend her kingdom from an invasion of trolls – either the renegade dragon-rider, or the vampire lord.

This shouldn't be a problem, except that Aliana hates to make either Kelwyn or Varek feel unwanted. They're both such wonderful neighbors, and she's constantly assuring Kelwyn that he's the best dragon-rider ever to fly the skies. Varek doesn't seem to need much reassurance, but even so she makes a point of admiring his cape whenever she spots him in the forest at night. If you don't let people know you appreciate their good points, what right do you have to call yourself a princess?

Well, of course she has that right by birth, but Aliana is determined to earn the love of not only her kingdom, but the rest of the world as well. And here's a wonderful opportunity to show her people how much she cares.

Festivals with proclamations of how much Princess Aliana loves her kingdom are all very well and good, but helping repel the trolls is an even better show of concern.

The only problem is that she can't enlist both Kelwyn and Varek, given that they've each sworn to wipe one another from the face of the earth. Which is a shame, because they're both such wonderful people. All right, they might have their annoying little habits, but Aliana is willing to overlook an occasional dragon-scorched forest or peasant drained of blood in order to stay on good terms with her neighbors.

So things are looking tricky. But she can't let the trolls invade her kingdom, because then virtually every peasant and the entire forest would be lost. No, she'll have to choose an ally…and quickly.

Fortunately, both the dragon-rider and the vampire lord know she has their best interests at heart. She's invited them to dinner – separately, of course – any number of times, and she's spent hours admiring Kelwyn's new harness and Varek's favorite jewel. She knows they view her as a good neighbor, and now it's time to collect on all those years of friendship.

But when she learns that Kelwyn is off dragon-hunting and Varek is flying from castle to castle, Aliana is furious. How can they ignore the princess who always listens to their stories, always serves their favorite dishes, always remembers to send birthday greetings? What kind of payback is that for all her thoughtful attention?

It would serve them right if she sent the trolls after *them*! Although of course she won't do that, because they're really such wonderful people….

= = = = = = = = =

Now, here's our cowboy facing off against the cattle rustlers. Buck is a Two, and he shouldn't have any problem rounding up enough friends to help in this struggle. Buck has dozens of friends, not only on the Triple C but also in town and at the Triple D. Even the Triple E, come to think of it, because he's made a point of meeting everyone in the county and paying his respects.

So it's just a matter of keeping an ear out, learning where the rustlers plan to strike next, and enlisting whoever's handy when the time comes. Buck will cover the south forty himself, because that'll be the toughest job and he wouldn't ask any friend to take on such a chore.

But riding the south forty alone is kind of disquieting. Sure, he knows the other cowboys are out there somewhere…but what if they already caught the rustlers, struck up a poker game in the bunkhouse, and forgot to tell him about it?

Naw, that's crazy. These people are Buck's friends, and they wouldn't do a fool thing like that.

Unless Jeb suggested it. Buck's never been too sure about Jeb, who once accused him of "acting all nice even when you don't mean it." What kind of accusation is that, anyway? Making it sound like Buck's just pretending to be friendly, like he doesn't *really* think all his fellow ranch hands are the greatest cowboys in the West?

Okay, so maybe once in a blue moon he'd rather go drinking alone than with a whole group of friends, but that's no way to keep people around. And it's not like he wants to go drinking alone all that often, anyway.

Not when there's a whole town full of people who need a friend like Buck. The sheriff, the schoolmarm, the barber, the saloon keeper, they all like having him around. That's fine with Buck. It doesn't bother him, knowing folks need his advice or his help or his horsemanship.

That's what friends are for, helping each other out, and if it seems like Buck does more helping than anyone else, so what? Friends don't keep score.

So it's all the more crazy for him to be worried about them starting up a poker game without him. Not even Jeb would do a thing like that, and if he ever suggested it the other cowboys would shout him down. It's just, riding the south forty alone all night isn't Buck's idea of a great time. Sure would be nice if he had someone else along.

Somebody who needed a little help. Somebody he could look out for, a greenhorn who might be nervous or worried about the trail. Someone who needs a friend like Buck.

= = = = = = = =

Let's take a look at the teenager whose only friend finds a buried treasure in the family's backyard.

As a Two, Jamie's first thought is automatically of how this discovery will help the family. Mom can get that new dishwasher, Dad can quit working overtime. They can buy out the pet store for Bowser, although that might be overdoing things a little.

"What about you?" Kelly asks. "What'll you do with your share?"

Jamie is taken aback. Of course it makes sense that everyone gets a share, but that's not what buried treasure is about. It's about making other people happy, showing them how much Jamie matters to the family, not going shopping for a new car.

Not that Jamie even wants a new car, really. You have to be sixteen to drive it, and it'd be pointless to let a new car sit waiting around in the garage all that time. Kelly's already making big plans for a silver Porsche, though, and worrying that it'll set a bad example if Jamie doesn't buy a car as well. "My parents will say that if you're not doing it, why should I?"

Here's a real dilemma. Maybe the kindest thing to do would be to help Kelly out by deciding on a new car as well. But what kind of message does that send? Greedy teenagers thinking only of themselves. Jamie's not that kind of person, and the very idea is appalling.

All right, then, maybe the only solution is to talk Kelly into donating the money to charity. The whole treasure. After all, they're the ones who found it, so they should get to announce where it goes. Except that decision sounds equally tough. New playground equipment for the school? More hot meals for the elderly? Extra doctors for the hospital? Too many good causes are making Jamie's head swim.

The only consolation is that no matter which one they pick, there'll be a big celebration in the community. People will realize that Jamie and Kelly aren't just typical selfish kids; they're more concerned with helping others. Especially Jamie, because Kelly wasn't the one who came up with the idea of a charity donation.

Kelly, though, isn't about to give up on the idea of a silver Porsche. "You can give your half to charity if you want, but I'm still going for the car." Which presents a whole new problem. What if Kelly decides this whole thing was just a means of earning the town's Most Helpful Citizen award? Because, without Kelly, the award won't mean nearly as much....

= = = = = = = =

Finally, the career woman who hires a detective to find the baby she gave up for adoption 13 years ago. As a Two, Anne might have had any number of reasons for the adoption – let's say she knew her parents had enough to deal with, and that she couldn't support the baby on her own, so the most loving thing to do was give the child to a caring family.

But now she's discovered some rare disease which the adoptive parents must be warned about, and all her nurturing instincts come into play. This isn't selfish, seeking out her daughter, this is an act of kindness to everyone involved. So what better reason to hire a detective and embark on a search for Emily?

She'll do whatever she can to help Craig with the search, and when they set off for the first potential city she offers to drive all night so he can get some sleep.

It surprises her when he insists that she needs her sleep, as well...Anne is used to looking out for other people rather than letting them look out for her. Well, sooner or later Craig will realize that she doesn't need any pampering. She's happier taking care of others.

But for some reason Craig won't accept that. He keeps trying to do things for her, buying her breakfast at the diner, taking a rest break before she's even mentioned feeling weary, and refusing to let her do more than her share of the driving. It's unnerving, being with someone who won't let her help. Anne is good at helping – that's what all her friends and co-workers like best about her – and she's happy to do it. Sitting back and letting someone help *her* is unnerving.

And just a little bit appealing.

No, that's a selfish way to think. Better to focus on what she can do for Craig. If he doesn't need her, fine, but surely Emily and the adoptive parents will need the kind of reassurance Anne's so good at. It's not like Craig *has* to need her, but she wishes he would.

Then they find Emily's family, and although the adoptive parents are politely grateful, they don't seem nearly as appreciative as Anne had expected. Of course it wasn't like she expected a brass band, but a little more thanks would have been nice. Craig, though, seems to think she's devastated by the entire event, and he insists on giving her dinner and a foot massage.

No, she can't accept it. She's getting far too close to needing this man, depending on him, and that's not how Anne wants to live. But somehow, with Craig, she's beginning to wonder.

Keep in mind that even if she does let Craig care for her, she's still a Two. A happier, healthier Two who's overcome the fatal flaw of pride – wanting to be essential to others rather than needing any help – but a Two nonetheless.

Nobody changes their type. They can change their outlook on life, they can change the traits which have kept them from being the best they can be, but their fundamental type never changes.

Because remember how all nine types can be terrific people? A happy ending just means that this particular type has found their best self. A tragic ending means they've found it and turned away. An either-way ending means they haven't found it yet…but maybe they will in the next story.

You're the writer. You can pick. And readers who share your view of the world will be delighted with whatever choice you make.

CHAPTER THREE

QUIZ

- ☐ Is achievement important to you?
- ☐ Are you confident about your abilities and skills?
- ☐ Are you a good sales person?
- ☐ Are you outgoing and popular?
- ☐ Do you work hard at accomplishing goals?
- ☐ Is image important to you?
- ☐ Are you usually busy?
- ☐ Do you hate to see jobs left undone?
- ☐ Do you value making a good first impression?
- ☐ Do you like to stand out in some way?

___ **TOTAL FOR THREE**

TYPE THREE: The Achiever, The Performer, Succeeder

You want somebody who can get the job done with fabulous style? With dazzling flair? With the kind of energy and enthusiasm that inspires everyone around them?

You want a Three.

There's nobody better at putting on a show. Whatever Threes undertake, they do with admirable grace and skill. There's no other choice – because they know that in order to be worthwhile, they must be constantly achieving great things.

Maybe they won't be the class president *and* prefect of the honor society *and* captain of the tennis team and head of the nature club and artist of the year and skater of the year and volunteer of the year and editor of the year. But if they aren't, it's sure not for lack of trying.

Threes work hard, and they make it look easy. They tend to believe that accomplishments matter more than feelings, that they're valued for what they do rather than for who they are.

The most well-adjusted Threes excel in every area they attempt, but go easy on themselves if they're less than outstanding in some other area. They might even laugh at themselves, and look great while doing it.

The less well-adjusted Threes will work hard at keeping up a perfect image of confidence, success and popularity. Because they're great at such missions, after a lifetime of performing to capacity, they'll have no trouble impressing people with their achievements…even when they dismiss any accolades with a beautifully humble smile.

But the work rarely stops. Threes are driven to be the best they can possibly be, and they're used to success.

From childhood on, they've known what it's like to be the Prince Charming or Golden Girl of whatever group they're in. And this makes them all the more self-confident, which makes them all the more capable of taking on new challenges and succeeding at each one.

If you took a stadium full of people and assigned the Ones to sit over there, the Twos over there, the Threes over there, and so on, it's a safe bet that the Three section would be filled with the best-looking people in the place. Threes are used to shining, used to excelling, and even those who might not technically be all *that* good-looking will give the impression they are.

Because their confidence is attractive. People see it and respond to it, and the Three responds by blooming under the light of their appreciation. A Three who was stranded on a desert island with no one to impress might have a hard time getting through the day…until inspired by the realization that "when I get off this island, the reporters will want to know how I managed."

Since Threes view themselves as having tremendous potential, they're not afraid of working to fulfill it. Long hours don't bother them. They're used to operating swiftly and efficiently, delivering whatever it takes to get the job done.

They're also gifted at sensing the reactions of others, and able to show whatever a crowd expects. This makes them outstanding performers – no matter whether it's acting or teaching or fund-raising or preaching or inspiring a team to new heights.

They live on a bigger scale than most people, always striving to make the most of what they were born with, or striving to present a perfect facade with no awareness of anything except the shell. Healthy or unaware, they consistently perform at a higher level.

And healthy Threes are a delight. Their strong self-esteem is fully justified, and they're happy to share their glowing talents with the world. A Three who's achieved Olympic gold medals in swimming will gladly teach the neighborhood kids to swim; a

Three who's mastered the culinary arts will give fabulous dinner parties.

Imagine a classic archetype of the golden warrior-poet-king, radiating goodwill and confidence and exuberant joy, and you've got a perfect picture of the Three.

Famous Threes

It's easy to envision famous Threes lighting up the stage and screen with their radiant personality and dramatic self-esteem. In fact, there are Hollywood stars whose characters pretty much always reflect that personality. Think Raquel Welch, Sharon Stone, Natalie Wood, Tom Cruise, Will Smith, Sylvester Stallone. Think Joan Crawford, Kathleen Turner, Demi Moore. All of whom audiences love to see again and again, giving off that wonderful Three aura of confidence and beauty and success.

Threes can be the personification of excellence, and when that excellence is paired with good-heartedness, it's impossible to resist.

People who didn't quite approve of that new-fangled music still had to admit there was something appealing about Elvis Presley. Diana Ross, Burt Reynolds, Wesley Snipes… Threes have a way of turning all eyes in their direction.

Even those who labor behind the scenes, like Henry Kissinger or Jimmy Carter, show up flawlessly when called to center stage. And it's not just politics and performing arts where Threes excel.

Look at Vince Lombardi, Dorothy Hammill and Michael Jordan. Look at Nora Ephron and F. Scott Fitzgerald. There's a larger-than-life quality to *all* Threes, which makes them fascinating to watch.

Not only are they driven to perform well, they're extremely good at persuading people to view things in a new light. Arnold Schwarzenegger, Oprah Winfrey, Oral Roberts and "walk on fire" coach Anthony Robbins are Threes who share their vision with the world. Regardless of what they're discussing, Threes have a gift for making us want to listen.

Three's Heroic Strengths

It's easy to create a Three whom readers will love. Threes at their best are tremendously admirable – the kind of person everyone wants to be, or at least to be with.

Threes who understand their own strengths and flaws are able to develop the best within themselves, and this makes them great role models.

Or great characters.

They're innately likeable, because they'll go out of their way to meet the expectations of everyone around them. If this means showing one side of their personality to one group, and another side to another group, no problem. They're good at recognizing what people want, and at presenting whatever the situation calls for.

Because Threes tend to feel they have to earn love, they'll do whatever it takes to be worthy of approval. Then, when they're rewarded with appreciation, they shine even brighter. It's a win/win situation, making everyone happy.

They thrive on knowing they're valued, and the happiness of such recognition makes them even more attractive, which makes people like them even more, which makes them even *more* charming...and the reinforcement continues in a mutually beneficial cycle.

No matter what the people around them value, Threes will find a way to deliver it. They'll work exceptionally hard to live up to expectations.

If they're in an academic environment, they'll write stellar term papers. If they're on a sports team, they'll practice their throws until midnight. If they're surrounded by sculptors, they'll either become great sculptors themselves or they'll become passionate fans of the art.

Best of all, this passion isn't just "put on" for the sake of winning friends. Or at least, not when the Three is a heroic character....

Three's Fatal Flaws

The negative aspect of Threes' need to meet expectations is that sometimes they care more about image than reality. If their friends adore gardening and they can't grow a single radish, they might go out and buy some home-grown radishes to arrange on their relish tray.

Even if they hate radishes, it's more important to keep up a good-gardener front than to acknowledge who they truly are… because what if people didn't *like* who they truly are?

Losing track of their real self is the greatest danger for Threes. When someone is used to being admired for success after success, it's easy to believe that nothing counts except achievement.

So doing whatever it takes to maintain a successful facade seems better than indulging any personal preferences or acknowledging any private feelings. Forget about those. Just keep up the image, just get things done proficiently, and disregard everything else.

It's important, in keeping up a good image, for the Three to appear successful at all times. So if there's any worry about failing at a project, better to ignore that. Better not to ask for help. Better to give the impression of having everything lined up perfectly than to risk any loss of face.

You can see how someone who spends a lifetime in that position could easily lose track of any inner feelings, any core beliefs. If the stellar facade becomes all there is, it makes more sense to value the appearance of popularity and credibility rather than actual intimacy and authenticity.

So a Three who finds it hard to live up to the incredibly high expectations of constant success (whether it's a real demand or just a perceived demand) can wind up losing any sense of self, and instead devote every scrap of energy to the effort of looking wonderful at all times.

No matter what the cost.

Threes As Children

It's easy to spot a Three on the playground or in the classroom. They're the ones other children look to for cues on what to wear, who to sit by, when to get in line. They know what makes the best impression, and they're usually the most popular kids in the class.

Teachers love Threes, because they're always attuned to expectations. They want to excel, and that means paying attention to lectures, turning in homework on time, doing extra-credit assignments, and bringing in the biggest and brightest apples. Threes make terrific group leaders, because they can inspire their team and talk people into greater achievements than anyone would have dreamed possible with some lesser leader at the helm.

When teachers or parents are proud of them, Threes are in heaven. Parents may find it hard to encourage their little Three to relax, stop and smell the roses, but these children can get stressed from being "on" too many hours a day. It's good for them to know that they're loved regardless of whether or not they collected the most awards.

A young Three who's faced with some difficulty might not ask for help, because the desire to appear competent could mean denying any problems along the way.

Not only will these budding stars work to appear competent at all times, but they'll usually display flawless manners... making them a pleasure to show off to neighbors and doting grandparents.

If they show any flaw, it may be a tendency toward arrogance (looking down on less successful siblings or classmates) or it may be their increasing demands for attention to reassure them that yes, they're still valued by the people whose approval matters most.

Threes At Work

Any boss will be glad to have a new Three on the job, because Threes go out of their way to acquire whatever skills they'll need to succeed. They frequently identify with their work so completely that they'll introduce themselves with their profession: "Hi, I'm Kerry, I'm in marketing for Acme Dynamics."

If Kerry's in charge of the marketing department, you can bet it'll be the best-run marketing department in town. Maybe not the best in terms of picky details, but far and away the best in terms of how good the projects look.

Threes are great at focusing on the big picture, working with feverish energy until the goal is achieved. Action is what matters, not philosophy.

This makes them an inspiration to co-workers, because they have the ability to sense what everyone in the group wants and offer a rallying spirit that makes teammates confident of success.

If they're given some new assignment, they'll want to start work immediately. "Let's get this *done!*" If they need to learn some new skills, they'll want to know how it applies to the job at hand. "Let's look at what we can *use!*" And if they wind up in a performance review, they might be more concerned with their own performance than with the finished product…unless they're responsible for the entire project.

When it's time for a Three's annual vacation, odds are that the job won't be left behind for long. Anytime they're not being productive, Threes feel lazy and uneasy. They'd far rather bring along work projects than spend a week relaxing on the beach. Just the kind of employee every boss loves!

Threes In Relationships

Because Threes aren't always aware of their own feelings, they may take their cue from those around them. If someone calls them "the perfect match" or "my dream date," they're willing to go along. And millions of people dream about a certain Three as their ideal match, because who can resist someone as talented and charming and good-looking as a Three?

It's only natural that Threes get used to being accepted and even admired, and if that admiration is withdrawn they may feel stricken. "What did I do wrong?"

But they won't let themselves worry for too long, not if such worry contradicts their image of confident well-being. Instead they'll deny any negative feelings, and focus on the positive. Happy people are more attractive, and Threes feel most alive when they're attractive to someone else.

Since they're used to putting their best efforts into succeeding at whatever they undertake, they'll put tremendous effort into maintaining great relationships. Whether a relationship is shallow and surface, or well-rounded and deep, depends on how secure the Three is about revealing any weakness or flaw.

In any case, Threes won't hesitate to take responsibility for making their mates feel good. Action is what counts, and they'll deliver whatever action – a dozen roses, a candlelit dinner, a night at the opera – will create the greatest happiness.

A relationship based on shared activity or common goals is one any Three will love. They'll gladly put their enthusiasm and dedication to work on having fun with their partners, creating great memories with their friends.

And if they're lucky, their partners and friends will let them know that simply *being*, with no need for *doing*, is enough to earn them all the love they could ever want.

Three's Individual Subtype

For a Three, self-preservation is all about security. This may be embodied by a corner office, by trophies testifying to significant achievements, or by inclusion in the decade's directory of Great Performers. But the most commonly sought security is material goods…and it can be hard for the Three to feel certain of having enough. If a million-dollar savings account doesn't ensure the desired level of security, the only option is to try for two million.

In a materialistic society, where individual value is often measured in terms of wealth, it's logical for Threes to take money as the standard by which they measure their own worth. But of course it's also possible that they'll measure their security in terms of health – making every effort to stay in good shape – or in terms of skills, taking classes at every opportunity to ensure staying on top of their field.

Threes who focus on self-preservation may not be quite as outgoing as other Threes, who need the active participation of their group or intimate relationships to assure them of their own success.

But they'll still be outstanding team players, willing to do whatever it takes to deliver a superior performance, because only by superior performance can they ensure the security they need. No matter how that security is measured, whether in wealth or accolades or personal ability, the self-preservation Threes will do their best to reach the highest levels they can possibly attain.

Three's Intimacy Subtype

Threes who value intimacy are most likely to seek it from romantic partners, because they're attractive enough to take their pick. Movies and books and TV shows constantly display the latest standards of what constitutes a perfect romantic partner, so the relational-subtype Threes need only look around them to see what it'll take to deliver a great performance.

If that's all the partner wants, the relationship can work just fine with the Three simply going through the correct motions. And a Three who feels uneasy about exposing personal emotions, which might not be as attractive as a perfect surface, may shy away from partners who want a more genuine connection. After all, there's a lot at risk.

If someone rejects the facade, it's easy to shrug and move onto the next candidate. But if someone rejects a Three's true self, there's no way to call that relationship a success.

Other types regret a failed relationship, too, but failure is even more appalling to a Three who's spent a lifetime in pursuit of constant success.

This passion for success makes them all the more determined to work at creating a great relationship, once they've set their sights on it. Threes aren't afraid of hard work, and they won't hesitate to meet the challenge of figuring out what their partner wants…then delivering it with all the charm they possess.

Three's Social Subtype

Threes whose main focus is on the society surrounding them will naturally be very conscious of what that society wants. Status and prestige become important, and the best way to achieve those is to meet and exceed whatever standards the group holds.

> **Since the worst imaginable situation for a Three is to be viewed as some anonymous nobody or "just one of the crowd," having the right credentials matters. Belonging to the right group matters. Being friends with the right people matters.**

Societal-subtype Threes are great at determining what the group values, and living up to that norm. This makes them wonderfully skilled at adapting to new situations, and if they wind up moving from Timbuktu to Tahiti, they'll have no problem scoping out the standards of their new group.

They can get along with virtually anyone, which makes them prized companions. What group *wouldn't* love to have a well-spoken, multi-talented, accommodating member who contributes an abundance of energy and enthusiasm to their society?

A Three who values practical logic will focus on furthering the group's goals; a Three who values personal warmth will focus on bolstering harmony within the group. Either way, they'll be more than welcome – and they'll thrive in a group which values them for their skilled contributions.

Threes With Other Types

Threes are great at getting along with other types just fine, but that doesn't provide much conflict for an author. Instead, take a look at what can go wrong when a Three encounters any of the nine types.

Three & One

Three wants to get this done in a blaze of glory by Friday; One wants to get it done right no matter how long that takes. Three leaps into action; One pulls back. Each feels impatient and frustrated: "Doesn't this person *get* it?"

Three & Two

Three has a project; Two wants to offer support. Three's too busy for support right now. "I'm fine, go take care of someone else." "But I'm here for *you*!" "I've got to get this done." "You won't let yourself need anyone."

Three & Three

He's got a big show to put on. She's got an award to accept. "Gotta get together one of these days." Both incredibly busy. Okay, the 26th. His club has better food. Hers has better views. Who'll show up later? Who'll look the best?

Three & Four

Three cares more about how the relationship looks. Four cares more about how it feels. Four wants Three to share feelings, no matter how painful or deep. Three would rather maintain a smooth and shallow surface.

Three & Five

Time for Three's inauguration as new mayor; Five shows up late because things got busy in the lab. Three demands, "Don't you appreciate the importance of my work?" Five retorts, "Don't you appreciate the importance of *mine*?"

Three & Six

"This," says Three, "is the greatest plan ever." Six asks, "What about this detail?" "Aw, don't worry about it." "But something could go wrong." "Come on, you're not looking at the big picture." "You're not looking at the details."

Three & Seven

They're both big-picture thinkers. They both enjoy planning swell activities. But either one can get wrapped up in something which results in ignoring the other, and feel frustrated when the other doesn't *get* their excitement.

Three & Eight

"Let's do it this way." "No, this way." "My way is better." "No, my way is better." "The whole point is, don't you want to be the best?" "Yes, that's why we need to do it this way." "No, that's why we need to do it *my* way."

Three & Nine

Three wants Nine's opinion on a new first-day-on-the-job suit. "Looks fine to me," says Nine. "No, come on, this is important." "I said it looked fine." "You're not really concentrating. Don't you understand how important this is?"

You see how none of these is a life-and-death conflict? But each one can be intensified or relieved, depending on where you are in the story.

Some conflicts may strike you as overly dramatic or overly boring. That's okay. That's a clear sign that your story doesn't *need* such a conflict. You may have enough conflict already. If you do need more, though, it's a safe bet that at least one of these examples will spark some ideas. And that's where the fun begins.

Scenarios With Threes

No matter what kind of story you're telling, the characters' personality types will make a difference in the conflict that arises. Here are examples of five stories – about a detective, a princess, a cowboy, a teenager and a career woman – where the protagonist will come into conflict because of his or her enneagram type.

= = = = = = = = =

Let's start with the cop trying to track down a blackmailer who's threatening the arrogant father-in-law of his beloved daughter. Jack Warner is a Three.

So he's got all kinds of reasons for wanting to catch this blackmailer. First, it's part of his job and he's always given the best possible performance to whatever police department he works for. Second, his daughter needs help and he's always given the best possible performance when it comes to looking out for his family. Third, he wouldn't mind showing Karen's father-in-law that even though he might not have a mansion and yacht, he's got a laudable track record when it comes to catching criminals.

Great incentive to track down the blackmailer. And Jack has some useful assets on his side. He's good at getting information from people; he knows how to persuade bank clerks and receptionists and informants to support his mission. He brings the same energy and enthusiasm to this job as he brings to everything else he undertakes, making co-workers excited about working late to send him reports. He's even good at TV interviews, lighting up the screen as he describes the suspects to watch for.

But what if his usual outstanding work isn't generating the results everyone expects? Bad enough that the chief of police is starting to grumble, but even worse is that he's letting down his daughter. How can he possibly fail at the most important assignment of his life?

There's gotta be some angle he hasn't thought of. So maybe while having dinner with Karen and her in-laws that night, Jack implies that he has a secret lead just to keep everyone feeling confident. (A lead could pop up any minute, so it's not like he's lying…just making things cleaner.) And maybe when a fellow cop offers some assistance, implying that Jack needs all the help he can get, Jack insists – with the breezy confidence everyone expects from him – that he's got everything under control.

But at some point, Jack will come face to face with the fact that his charming, successful facade has an element of deception. Maybe he'll admit to Karen that he's terrified of failing her, and she'll assure she loves him no matter what. Or maybe he won't admit it, or maybe he won't believe her, and will keep trying to perform better still – until he realizes that love doesn't have to be earned.

Maybe then he'll relax enough to catch the blackmailer, or let some other cop take the credit, or maybe not. It's all up to you!

= = = = = = = =

Next comes the princess trying to choose the best ally to defend her kingdom from an invasion of trolls – either the renegade dragon-rider, or the vampire lord.

As a Three, Aliana is pretty sure she can enlist the help of anyone she wants. She's used to persuading people, and she knows the dragon-rider will be impressed with her crossbow skills, while the vampire lord will be enamored with her jewels.

Maybe she's secretly terrified of the trolls, but terror is so unattractive that she can't possibly reveal that to a potential ally. For that matter, she can't reveal it to anyone in the kingdom, because who wants a princess sniveling about things?

No, her only hope for defending her people is choosing the right ally, but neither one of her choices is proving cooperative. Aliana's getting frustrated, knowing she doesn't have the skills to train an entire army in three days, and wishing her lessons had included more military strategy than magic. Of course she's kept up her magic, because it's important to be good at everything she touches, but that won't repel the invaders.

Maybe, though, she can use it to win the allegiance of the dragon-rider. Until now he's insisted that he won't join forces unless she explains every weakness in her castle, which she refuses to do. Her people deserve to be proud of their kingdom, and pointing out flaws is no way to keep up the peasants' spirits.

But if she can make Kelwyn fall in love with her, then she won't have to expose any weaknesses. Maybe the magic works, and Aliana wins Kelwyn's cooperation. Or maybe it fails right before the big battle, and she has to choose between losing her only ally against the trolls, or losing her pride by revealing the castle's weaknesses. Maybe she decides to enlist the vampire lord instead, but the peasants are aghast at the idea of her inviting Varek to dinner.

No matter what she does, she can't maintain the image everyone expects of a princess, and she's about ready to give up and surrender to the trolls.

As a Three, though, she's not going to let such a failure happen. Maybe she'll redouble her efforts at magic. Maybe she'll decide that it's worth giving up her perfect image in order to achieve peace for the kingdom. Maybe she'll ride into battle and become the subject of legends for the next few millennia. Your story. Your princess. Your pick.

= = = = = = = =

Now, here's our cowboy facing off against the cattle rustlers. Buck is a Three, which makes it surprising that he'd choose a job which involves a lot of solitude. But we can figure he's easily the most popular cowboy in the bunkhouse, and the other ranch hands look up to him as the kind of guy who can solve any problem.

Buck, of course, feels the same way. He's used to being good at whatever he does – nobody on the Triple C can ride faster, shoot straighter, round up more cattle in a day on the range. So picking off these cattle rustlers shouldn't be any big deal for someone who succeeds at every mission that comes his way.

Except, for some reason, he can't seem to catch the rustlers. This is getting to be a problem, because his reputation is at stake. What kind of cowboy can't pick off a few lousy cattle rustlers, for pete's sake?

Frustration isn't something he's used to, though, and Buck quickly dismisses any suspicion that he might not be up to the job.

No, it's just a matter of working harder. Staying out later, enlisting a few other ranch hands to cover the south forty. Kind of thing he can do with one hand tied behind his back, because he's the best cowboy on the Triple C, bar none.

But the cattle are still disappearing.

Now Buck's really starting to worry, and he's not used to worrying. He's used to overcoming any problems through his own energetic, get-it-done-in-a-blaze-of-glory efforts. Maybe the town schoolmarm is suggesting he call in the local deputy, but Buck can't stand the idea of showing Miss Lillian any sign of incompetence. No, by golly, he needs some other solution. And suddenly it strikes him.

The problem isn't the rustlers. It's the way the ranch is laid out! All this time, he and the hands have been herding cattle from the mountains to the valley, when it'd make better sense to herd cattle from the valley to the mountains. That way the rustlers won't have a chance. None of this was Buck's failure, after all – it was a simple problem of range management, but he'll talk to the ranch owner and get things fixed. Problem solved.

Being a persuasive fellow, he might convince the owner to change how the ranch is laid out. But if that still doesn't stop the rustlers, Buck's in worse trouble than before. His entire reputation is on the line, here, so what's he gonna do? Admit he's failed? Tell the deputy he can't handle things? Pack up and move to Laramie? Plenty of people in Laramie looking for a good cowboy… What's he gonna do?

= = = = = = = =

Let's take a look at the teenager whose only friend finds a buried treasure in the family's backyard.

Normally a Three as popular as Jamie would have far more than one friend, but let's say this family is living way out in the country with no neighbors except Kelly. So when Kelly finds a cache of jewels in Jamie's backyard, there aren't a lot of people around clamoring for the story.

But of course Jamie sees the opportunity, here. A word to the town newspaper, and they'll be written up as Stars Of Tomorrow – students who donated a fortune to save the town hospital from closing. The only problem is that Kelly doesn't want any publicity. In fact, Kelly wants to keep the jewels a secret. So Jamie has a tough job ahead.

One solution would be to ignore Kelly's preference and simply alert the media. Not a very friendly thing to do, though, and Jamie sees that as more of a last resort than a first pick. You've got to look out for your friends, because where else can you find the kind of approval that gets you through an otherwise boring day?

Not that Jamie has much chance to be bored, what with swim team and honor society and first-chair violin, but once school lets out there's nobody around except Kelly. So alienating Kelly is a bad idea. Persuasion, that's the thing.

Maybe suggesting a visit to the almost-closed hospital will do the trick. Maybe if Kelly sees how desperate things are over there, making a huge donation will look like a better idea.

Jamie can already see the front-page headlines, already hear the reporters' admiring questions. "Weren't you even tempted to keep the fortune a secret?" (An easy one to answer, with the modest shrug that's proven so popular.) "No, taking care of people in need is the most important thing in the world." Then the smile. Ah, this'll be great.

But Kelly isn't playing along, which is baffling. How can anybody, even someone as shy as Kelly, pass up a chance like this? Jamie will take care of all the talking, nothing to worry about there. And it's so easy to see: the lights coming up on a national talk show about Teens Who Matter – wearing the blue sweater, probably, because that strikes just the right balance between earnest and carefree.

Besides, this really *is* the best thing for the town hospital. Hmm, what about an anonymous phone call to the newspaper editor? There's got to be some way to make things work out for everyone....

= = = = = = = =

Finally, the career woman who hires a detective to find the baby she gave up for adoption 13 years ago. As a Three, Anne might have had any number of reasons for the adoption – let's say she knew she wasn't yet capable of being the best possible mother, and the baby deserved a perfect family.

But now she's discovered some rare disease which the adoptive parents must be warned about, and she can't help admitting she's curious to see the child she gave birth to. Not to interfere with Emily's life – she knows that wouldn't be fair, but still it's her own flesh and blood out there. Of course she'd at least like to *see* her daughter.

She's aware that the detective is impressed with her from the moment they meet. Nothing new there; men pretty much always find her attractive, and Anne knows how to leave them feeling good about the whole encounter. They smile at her, she smiles at them; everybody feels appreciated and goes home happy.

Craig, though, seems interested in more than just carefree chit-chat. She has the impression he wants to get to know *her*, which is a sweet idea but not terribly practical.

If he wants to swap life stories, okay, but getting into deep-seated hopes and dreams and fears just isn't her style. Better to keep things on the surface, where she *knows* she can make a good impression, than risk him being disappointed with anything more.

Yet when they discover that Emily's adoptive parents have left the state and Anne is devastated, Craig is right there with a shoulder to cry on. Crying is horribly unattractive, but he doesn't seem to mind. It's bizarre, though; here she is falling apart and the man still likes her? Maybe he has some kind of savior complex, but he's always seemed so normal….

Maybe things get even more complicated when they find Emily, and Anne sees in her daughter the same passion for excellence she's always shown the world. But Emily's craving for approval startles her – doesn't this child realize she's wonderful even without bringing home straight A's? Maybe Craig points out that here's proof this is the right child, because she clearly possesses her mother's need for validation.

Maybe she decides Craig is just too invasive, writes him a generous check and waves goodbye. Maybe she acknowledges the resemblance but insists Emily has exactly the right outlook on life, because achievement is all you can ever really count on. Or maybe she takes the risk of opening her heart to Craig, gambling that love might be possible even if she's occasionally less than perfect.

Or maybe she decides something else. Whatever you want.

Keep in mind that even if she does opt to risk showing Craig her true self, she's still a Three. A happier, healthier Three who's overcome the fatal flaw of deception – putting on a show of perfection for everyone around her at every possible moment – but a Three nonetheless.

Nobody changes their type. They can change their outlook on life, they can change the traits which have kept them from being the best they can be, but their fundamental type never changes.

Because remember how all nine types can be terrific people? A happy ending just means that this particular type has found their best self. A tragic ending means they've found it and turned away. An either-way ending means they haven't found it yet…but maybe they will in the next story.

You're the writer. You can pick. And readers who share your view of the world will be delighted with whatever choice you make.

CHAPTER FOUR

QUIZ

- ☐ Do you frequently feel that nobody understands you?
- ☐ Do you sometimes wonder when you'll find your one great love?
- ☐ Are you exceptionally sensitive to critical remarks?
- ☐ Do you find yourself envying what others have?
- ☐ Is it important to you to feel that you fit in?
- ☐ Do you sometimes find yourself drawn to melancholy thoughts?
- ☐ Do you think you have deeper feelings than the average person?
- ☐ Are you troubled by fears of abandonment?
- ☐ Do you hunger for the perfect soul mate?
- ☐ Do you sometimes feel like an outsider, even with your friends?

___ **TOTAL FOR FOUR**

TYPE FOUR: The Artist, The Romantic, The Individual

Fours have big feelings. Huge, vast, sweeping emotions. They see the best in any drama, any tragedy, any instance of falling in love – anything that offers room for the full depth of their powerful feelings.

The only problem with everyday life is that it's frequently too ordinary. Too flat. Fours are very comfortable with their own emotions, and very much in tune with what they're feeling at any given time.

They're bewildered by people who hide their feelings behind a mask – why would anyone want to do that? How can people not want to share their greatest moments of truth and beauty and universal understanding with the rest of the world?

Fours are the most self-aware of all the types. It's their greatest gift, because it gives them the ability to turn their imagination and feelings into glorious works that reflect a deep understanding of the human condition.

It's also their greatest curse, because it can leave them hungering for some missing ingredient that keeps their life from being utterly perfect…a state they *know* is possible because they can envision it so clearly.

With the ability to envision life as it should be – life at its most grand and purposeful and powerful and dramatic – Fours are sometimes disappointed when reality doesn't measure up. Sometimes they blame themselves, suspecting that "if only I were a better and greater person, then life would live up to my dreams. Not just my life, but the life of the whole world!" Fours have big, *big* feelings.

It's the desire to understand and express these feelings that leads so many Fours to become what enneagram theorist Tom Condon calls "translators of humanity." Fours are often involved in the arts – painting, writing, acting, composing, bringing their deeply-felt perceptions to life. They make outstanding teachers, counselors and spiritual advisors, because they're so easily able to recognize and give voice to universal truths that frequently go unnoticed by other types.

No wonder Fours feel special. They're more emotionally honest than any other type, and yet they don't always get the acknowledgement they yearn for when they share their sweeping emotional ups and downs.

That's why so many of them turn to art as a vehicle for expression, because it allows them to reveal themselves to the world.

And a Four who lacks the skill to create sculptures or write plays will still have a deep appreciation for beauty. In fact, this Four will likely be an art collector or have a fabulously decorated home or wear distinctively stylish clothing. The desire for grand harmony is going to come out somewhere.

Sometimes it comes out in idealistic thinking. Fours have a strong sense of how wonderful life *could* be, and can be highly disappointed when reality doesn't live up to their keen imagination. At such times they may retreat into their own feelings, hurt that nobody seems to understand them…and possibly appreciating the tragically romantic quality of such fierce disappointment.

If a Four has some personal defect, it may become a source of pride. "Nobody else has ever suffered the way I do." "The world will never realize what it costs me to get up in the morning." At the same time, though, they take just as much pride in their personal strengths. "Mrs. Smith has never met anyone as understanding as I am." "I have so incredibly much to give the world."

Because understanding comes so easily to them, many Fours take it for granted. They have a tremendous gift for recognizing the feelings of others, and for offering wholehearted sympathy – even empathy – when someone is feeling low. Most people would be uncomfortable if a friend broke down sobbing in their kitchen, but

Fours are never afraid of emotion. Emotions are the essential element of life, and life without big, passionate ups and downs is just too flat. What matters most is feelings...and nobody understands that better than a Four.

Famous Fours

Because Fours are drawn to the arts, it's no surprise that drama and creativity are the hallmarks of almost every well-known Four.

Fours who act are usually known for their ability to play a wide variety of characters. They're never just "a tough guy" or "a beautiful girl" – there's always more depth to their roles. Look at Laurence Olivier, Marlon Brando and Johnny Depp. Judy Garland, Robert De Niro and Liam Neeson. They might excel at playing the role of a Four – someone who feels different, set apart, lonely and tormented – like Winona Ryder or James Dean.

Equally famous are literary characters who embody Four's ability to mourn for the unattainable, especially unattainable love.

Cyrano de Bergerac, the Phantom of the Opera, and the Hunchback of Notre Dame all reflect the Four gift for idealizing a perfect love, and savoring the melancholy pleasure of contemplating what can never be.

Melancholy is a state most Fours know well. In fact, it's frequently expressed in their artwork. Vincent Van Gogh may be the most famous, but that same tragic and romantic quality is visible in the photographs of Diane Arbus, the films of Ingmar Bergman, and the music of Kurt Cobain.

Music is a favorite means of self-expression, because it conveys deep emotion so well. Listen to Billie Holliday, Leonard Cohen or Jim Morrison. Paul Simon, Janis Joplin and James Taylor. Fours can bleed more profoundly than any other type.

Which is also what makes them such tremendously evocative writers. Like Anne Rice, who gives the sweeping emotions of a Four to her most popular characters. Like Tennessee Williams, Virginia Woolf and Robert James Waller...none of whom holds back from exploring big, *big* feelings.

Four's Heroic Strengths

Anyone who creates grand, vivid fantasies as often as a Four does will have a powerful imagination. This feeds the richness of their emotions, which makes them all the more artistic. And because they're not afraid to explore their own feelings, Fours possess a wealth of intuition when it comes to others' feelings.

They're more perceptive than other types, and can be wonderfully warm and supportive to anyone who needs a shoulder to cry on. Fours know the importance of a shoulder to cry on better than most, because they so often need it themselves. This gives them a gentle compassion that friends appreciate, even if they don't always return the favor as fully as the Four might wish.

Being keenly aware of feelings increases the Four's capacity for creativity, and they can find meaning in virtually everything. That gift enhances their sense of intuition, and well-adjusted Fours have such a clear perspective that they often see the humor someone else might miss.

At the same time, they're able to see greater details of a neighbor's personality, greater visions of the future with a new friend, greater tragedy in a lost pencil…any event that might elicit a minor response from other types can easily generate a major response from Fours.

They take things personally, which makes them strongly individualistic. And because they're usually more in touch with their impulses, they can translate their feelings into self-expression with very little trouble.

Fours appreciate the unique – not only in themselves, but in others as well. Whether they share their witty insights with the world or with a few close friends, they have a knack for spotting what's special and celebrating it with all the passion they possess.

Four's Fatal Flaws

Fours are so comfortable with expressing their feelings, so accustomed to sharing their authentic selves with the world at large, that they can sometimes leave other types wishing for some nice "small talk" about the weather.

But what can you expect from someone with big feelings? A Four can't really turn off the emotional awareness that permeates every aspect of life, and sometimes that becomes overwhelming. The only way to deal with such a burden is to retreat from the world – but this can lead to loneliness, which is every bit as painful.

So here's our Four, buffeted by a constant flood of emotions and keenly aware that nobody else in the room seems bothered by Janet's tight smile and Leo's overly boisterous laugh.

"Why am I so different?" the Four laments. "Even though I like being special, I wish I could be as relaxed as George and as hospitable as Kate."

You see the fatal flaw creeping in here? It's envy. And it makes sense that someone who can easily imagine a truly perfect world, yet who can also see how a particular situation doesn't equal that vision, will be plagued by envy of happier people whenever reality doesn't live up to the fantasy.

Fours who haven't yet learned to set aside this envy can wind up losing perspective, becoming self-conscious, or feeling that because they're *so* special and *so* disappointed by life, they need more privileges and more sympathy and more freedom to do as they please.

On the other hand, Fours who recognize their fatal flaw are able to counteract it by taking a step back and looking at what they *do* have, rather than at what they don't. These Fours can even laugh at themselves, and get back to enjoying their big feelings in a very, very, very big way.

Fours As Children

When any child doesn't fully embody the absolute best of Mom and Dad, it's only natural that the parents will be a little disappointed. Most parents will honor and recognize that such differences are part of life, and the child won't be too worried about it.

Unless, of course, the child is a Four. A baby Four can sense every feeling of every person standing around the crib, and will automatically pick up the notion that today's mission is to fully embody the absolute best of Mom and Dad.

Which would be just fine, if this Four were an identical copy of both parents. But since that's flat-out impossible, we know what's going to happen. The Four is going to worry about being a disappointment, about being abandoned by the big people, about never really belonging in the world.

No wonder so many Fours feel misunderstood, lonely or shy. With their intuitive ability to read the emotions of those around them, they're keenly aware of any differences between themselves and their caretakers.

As they grow into the teenage years, they may cherish and even exaggerate those differences – whatever it takes to achieve a sense of independence – but very young Fours appreciate all the loving reassurance they can get. "You're wonderful the way you are. You're special the way you are."

Their well-developed sensitivity gives these children a sense of compassion and altruism which can work wonders at building relationships with those in need. A Four who visits an elderly neighbor, or adopts an abandoned puppy, or makes get-well cards for hospital patients, will enjoy the satisfaction of feeling appreciated...as well as the happy emotions of a brand new friend.

Fours At Work

It's no surprise that Fours prefer work which is emotionally intense. If they're assigned to tighten bolts on an assembly line, they'll be much happier with co-workers going through an adoption or divorce or pending prom date. If they're working in a therapy clinic or emergency room, they'll thrive on the very drama that can drive other types into less demanding fields.

Being naturally creative, Fours want work that lets them produce something distinct. Tightening bolts is too ordinary to be satisfying, but what if every third bolt were painted yellow? Fours will come up with visions for making their assembly line – or their bakery, classroom, office or auto repair shop – a more vivid, unique place to work.

Once they come up with a vision, though, they want some acknowledgment for it.

Fours don't want to be "just part of the team," not when they can be regarded as shining stars. They want to be valued as distinctive individuals who bring something special to the job.

Because they enjoy drama, Fours thrive on challenge. They'd far rather be involved in starting a new project than on carrying out the everyday details. If things are always ordinary, what's the point in showing up at work? Restless Fours might stir up controversy, just to have *something* happening on the job, but they'd be equally happy with a demanding new assignment. Just as long as there's something to get excited about.

Fours who feel needed and appreciated at work are more likely to give it their best. A little recognition goes a long way – and if ever someone gets to wear a crown for the day, the happiest crown wearer will always be a Four.

Fours In Relationships

Because Fours are so free with their emotions, sharing feelings will be a big part of any relationship. They'll want someone who can appreciate the depth of their feelings, who can share the depth of their involvement.

The other person doesn't necessarily have to feel things as intensely as the Four does, but had better be willing to listen and sympathize and understand whatever the Four is feeling when they're together. And the other person should be honest about the effect of the Four's mood: "When you're all excited like that, I feel awed." "You seem so distraught, it makes me feel sad."

Dismissing the Four's feelings – "don't worry, things will look better in the morning" – may strike the Four as terribly cold or wretchedly indifferent, even when it's meant to be a helpful, caring response. There's no getting around the fact that Fours need time to process and express all the feelings that swirl through them, and anyone who's uncomfortable with that need will probably be unhappy with a Four.

But for people who appreciate the warmth of genuine empathy whenever they feel blue, who value the Four's gift for creativity and perception, who aren't afraid of showing their love, and who don't mind emotional ups and downs, a relationship with a Four will be tremendously satisfying. No other type offers such depth of feeling, nor such heartfelt involvement.

The key to enjoying time with Fours is to avoid letting their moods control you. (Or them!) If you can offer a new perspective on any situation while still making the Four feel valued, you'll be rewarded with all the dazzling joy, humor, artistic flair and creative self-expression that Fours bring to every single day of their life.

Four's Individual Subtype

Any Four who's concerned with self-preservation knows that the best way to preserve any great quality of life is to find constant stimulation. Intensity, even if it comes from disaster or catastrophe, is far preferable to the kind of dreary, mundane existence that makes life meaningless.

Birth is good. Death is good. Danger is good. This Four won't hesitate to plunge into a dangerous situation, to pull everyone through a crisis with sheer, determined perseverance.

The joy of taking risks is the emotional payoff that comes with them. It's hard to resist the dramatic glory of feeling like the center of attention.

So individual-subtype Fours will focus intently on issues that demand tremendous personal involvement. Maybe something creative, maybe something with an edge of danger, maybe something with an inherent potential for drama. Whatever they choose, they'll throw themselves into it wholeheartedly, ignoring everyday surroundings and ordinary necessities in passionate pursuit of their quest.

While they don't mind public adulation for saving the world, they don't want to be typecast, either. If someone says, "I know all about your type; you're a classic do-good hero," they'll probably rebel at the very idea. The thought of being cast in a mold is repugnant to Fours. They want the freedom to chart their own course and express themselves however they choose...in whatever grand fashion they think best.

Four's Intimacy Subtype

Fours with a relational subtype are all about – yep, you guessed it – relationships. Glorious, intense, unique relationships. They're attracted to the dream of a perfect love, and may spend a lifetime longing for Prince Charming or the Ideal Woman even if they're satisfied with the partner they've got. The unobtainable is just so much more exciting.

When life seems too ordinary, the dream of a soul mate becomes even more appealing. They may push their partner away, then struggle to repair the relationship, because that kind of angst is more fulfilling than a humdrum life together.

Such push-pull drama lets Fours retain a sense of control... and of distance.

Why is distance so important? Because Fours worry about not being special enough. If they let someone get close, and then fail to deliver the kind of passionate intensity they want from a partner – good heavens, they might not be the most important person in their partner's life. They might not be truly loved.

Looking around them, they can see plenty of people who seem to have the same kind of life as theirs...but those people seem just a bit more happy. A bit more interesting. A bit more fulfilled. And relationship-subtype Fours know what the problem is: their own relationships aren't everything they should be. Time to suffer and withdraw. Time to reunite and celebrate. Time for another round of big, big emotions!

Four's Social Subtype

Every society has its own ideals, and social-subtype Fours are always worried about measuring up. They're good at analyzing their place in the world, and conscious of any areas where they don't fully live up to the social norms.

Not being included in the group is devastating, and a Four will do anything to keep that from happening. They might turn on the charm, turn on the flash, make themselves impossible to ignore. Or they might ease back and fade into the woodwork until they can regain enough self-confidence to take their place again.

What matters is being valued by the group. No wonder they dream of great deeds that will earn them more status and recognition. No wonder they're quick to recognize put-downs.

If they can fill specific roles, like being the group's fashion advisor or expert on restaurants or the one people turn to for a shoulder to cry on, they're delighted. Now they can ensure that they matter.

Because Fours are so aware of how they fit into society, they know immediately where their social strengths and weaknesses lie. Of course they'll play up their strengths, but their weaknesses will be turned into colorful quirks. "Can you believe it? I *never* seem to have the right time!" Whatever the defect, it'll be presented with the Four's charming flair for drama…and for the romance of everyday life.

Fours With Other Types

Fours are great at understanding and empathizing with other types, but that doesn't provide much conflict for an author. Instead, take a look at what can go wrong when a Four encounters any of the nine types.

Four & One

Four wants to express emotions; One wants to control them. "But I'm just so upset!" "Come on, get hold of yourself. I'm upset, too, but you don't see me getting all whacked out." "You've never been in touch with your feelings."

Four & Two

Four is feeling melancholy, so Two offers a kindly pat on the back. "There, there, I'll make you some tea." "Tea won't help, I need to mourn." "But I want you to feel better." "Can't you just let me grieve?" "I don't understand." "You sure don't."

Four & Three

Four cares more about how the relationship feels; Three cares more about how it looks. Four wants Three to share feelings, no matter how painful or deep. Three would rather maintain a smooth and shallow surface.

Four & Four

If things are going badly, both Fours will blame themselves. This makes them feel worse, so they'll turn around and blame each other. Now they feel even worse, so they'll break apart. This makes them feel even worse…

Four & Five

Four is getting upset about a crisis with a friend; Five is detached. Four asks, "Don't you *care* about people?" "Sure, but you're being too dramatic." "You're being too aloof – you've never cared about me *or* my feelings!"

Four & Six

Four is excited about a new movie, but Six isn't: "I'm not so sure." "Oh, come on, take a risk." "Not all of us enjoy living on the edge." "But you need a little more drama in your life." "You've got more than enough drama for both of us."

Four & Seven

Four is in pain; Seven is feeling strangled and wants to get out. Four needs emotional sustenance which Seven can't provide: "I can't keep looking on the dark side." "If you cry with me we'll both feel better." "It won't work."

Four & Eight

An intense relationship, because both feel like they're above the rules. Four admires and envies Eight's emotional authenticity, Eight admires and envies Four's artistic creativity. But when they're angry, the sparks fly!

Four & Nine

Four wants Nine to be fully involved. "I *am* involved; I'm right here in the room with you." "But you're not showing me your deepest self." "I can't ever make you happy." "You could at least *try*." "It'll never be enough for you."

You see how none of these is a life-and-death conflict? But each one can be intensified or relieved, depending on where you are in the story.

Some conflicts may strike you as overly dramatic or overly boring. That's okay. That's a clear sign that your story doesn't *need* such a conflict. You may have enough conflict already. If you do need more, though, it's a safe bet that at least one of these examples will spark some ideas. And that's where the fun begins.

Scenarios With Fours

No matter what kind of story you're telling, the characters' personality types will make a difference in the conflict that arises. Here are examples of five stories – about a detective, a princess, a cowboy, a teenager and a career woman – where the protagonist will come into conflict because of his or her enneagram type.

= = = = = = = =

Let's start with the cop trying to track down a blackmailer who's threatening the arrogant father-in-law of his beloved daughter. Jack Warner is a Four, which means he's never been the kind of detective who relies solely on logic.

No, he trusts his instincts as well…and his instincts are telling him there's more to this blackmail story than meets the eye. Maybe

Karen's father-in-law has been throwing his weight around a little too freely; Jack can't be the only person who thinks this guy's a jerk. In any case, there could be something behind these threatening letters.

So what's he gonna do? He'll start by putting his people-skills to work, listening to everyone who might know something about the case. He can sense when someone's holding back, and that's served him well during his career. In fact, he's built a reputation for being able to break through to people whom other cops can't reach.

And here's his chance to shine. Ever since Karen left home with her new husband – a good guy, Jack knows he'll give her a decent life – he's kind of regretted that his daughter no longer has much use for good old Dad.

Not that he'd complain about it; Karen deserves to be happy. But this kind of detective work is something only *he* can do for her, and he's going to do it brilliantly.

Matter of fact, if the case is big enough, there could be a promotion involved. Captain Ryan notices great work, and Jack's about due for some recognition. Lee's been getting plenty of it, so have Taylor and Kane. But they don't bring the same kind of intuitive understanding to the job that Jack brings every day.

All he needs is the right lead. Then Karen will be awed. His son-in-law will be grateful. Ryan will be impressed. No question, everybody will agree Jack's got some exceptional talent.

The only problem is, that vision doesn't seem to be taking shape. He's having a hard time cracking this case, and it's his own damn fault. What's wrong with him, anyway? Not only is he letting down his family and his fellow cops, he's missing out on what should have been the best job of his career.

So what's he gonna do? Wallow in misery, maybe. Give up hope of ever solving this case, knowing it's a failure he can never overcome. Or maybe he'll recognize how easy it is for a guy like himself to lose perspective, and get back to work with renewed determination. Whatever works for your story will work for Jack.

= = = = = = = =

Next comes the princess trying to choose the best ally to defend her kingdom from an invasion of trolls – either the renegade dragon-rider, or the vampire lord.

As a Four, Aliana is invigorated by the challenge. Finally, a chance to live every moment as if it were her last! No more dull days at court, no more looking out the tower window wishing for the love of her life to ride up on a white horse. (No telling who that will be, but surely he'll arrive someday.)

Right now, though, she has a vital mission, and she's ready to face it with flags flying high.

Her flags fly high all the way to the dungeon of the vampire lord, who seems unimpressed with her plea for assistance. Well, fine. She has other options, so who *cares* about a stupid vampire lord anyway? As if she ever took Varek seriously in the first place! No, clearly her best hope is with the dragon-rider, and she should have talked to him first.

It's important to make him realize she's not just some ordinary princess looking for a handout. This isn't the kind of visit he gets on a normal day. Once he sees her silver gown with the dramatic cluster of emeralds, Kelwyn will recognize that he's dealing with someone special.

But when he refuses to send his dragons into the fray, Aliana is devastated. This is a tragedy beyond anything she could have imagined – or, well, maybe not – but it's certainly a tragedy she wasn't expecting. The trolls are getting closer every minute, and now she can't count on either of her closest hopes? There's something wrong with this picture.

And, unfortunately, she knows what that is.

Herself.

If only she were more beautiful. If only she had the kind of pale skin and visible pulse it would take to win Varek's allegiance, or the kind of devil-may-care insouciance it would take to rouse Kelwyn's interest. Oh, she's failed miserably!

But after a few hours of grieving, knowing that nothing will ever go right again, she remembers another option. Trolls aren't known for their appreciation of beauty, but they've never before seen a kingdom like hers. If she raises blue and red flags throughout the woods, then gets enough peasants to scatter flowers along the road which circumvents the town, maybe she can save the day.

This is what life is all about, she tells herself, watching the army of trolls from the highest turret of the castle. No matter how things turn out, today will be a day of tremendous impact. She can hardly wait....

= = = = = = = =

Now, here's our cowboy facing off against the cattle rustlers. Buck is a Four, and we can assume that since he's chosen such a solitary job he's more concerned with self-preservation than with intimate relationships or social groups. But since the cattle rustlers are affecting his livelihood as well as that of the entire ranch, he's got to take some kind of action.

Okay, then. Not like he's afraid of facing some kind of challenge. Might be quite a showdown, come to think of it – already he can feel his blood pulsing faster. Just him and the lead rustler, squaring off outside the saloon. Buck's got a white hat, and surely the rustler will have a black one. Yeah, he can see it now.

He'll draw his gun first, but he won't fire. No, he'll just flick it out of the holster and hear the townspeople gasp. Miss Lillian, the schoolmarm, will probably faint. He might have to take her in his arms – but, no, wait, first he's gotta get rid of the rustler. *Then* see to Miss Lillian.

This'll be a great day, Buck knows. Not much breeze, but a rumble of thunder across the valley. Be nice if the lightning strikes at the exact moment he confronts the rustler...hell, it could happen. Probably will, in fact, because he's got the music in his blood today. Things are gonna work out real sweet.

Except, drat it, there's no sign of the rustlers on the south forty. He's all ready for action, and where are those lily-livered cowards? For that matter, where's Miss Lillian? It's not gonna be much of a showdown if she's stuck in the schoolhouse with the kids.

Well, maybe the gals at the saloon will faint when he squares off against the guy in the black hat, but that's not the way he saw it happening.

"You're a dreamer, Buck," his ma always told him. But what's wrong with dreaming? Gotta get through the day somehow, and watching a herd of cattle isn't exactly the most exciting way to pass the time. Sure, dreams can get you in trouble if you're caught by surprise in the middle of a stampede, but that's never happened to him.

And if it did, well, he's pretty sure Miss Lillian would never get over it. Probably spend the rest of her life grieving over the loss of her one true love....

That's not gonna happen, though. Just a matter of tracking down the rustlers and saving the day. White hat, gun at the ready. Yep, he can see it now.

= = = = = = = =

Let's take a look at the teenager whose only friend finds a buried treasure in the family's backyard. Jamie is a Four, and the drama of this discovery is a wonderful thing. Life's been a little flat lately, a little ordinary, and now this cache of emeralds means that things are going to get exciting.

The only problem is Kelly, who insists they keep it a secret until they can figure out who owns the rights to such treasure. Fine, Jamie understands there are legal details to sort through, but what about the fanfare? Why not take a few pieces to school and casually show them off? "Oh, just a little something I picked up this weekend."

But Kelly's being all picky about land deeds and the statute of limitations, and Jamie's getting annoyed. Here this terrific windfall has practically landed in their laps, so why not make the most of it?

Even if they don't get to keep the money, they can ride the excitement for a good week or two. What kind of friend can't understand the importance of making things special?

Come to think of it, maybe Kelly's never really *been* a true friend. Maybe all these years of going home together after school, catching each other up on missed TV shows, has all been a sham. Maybe Kelly thinks Jamie's too boring, or too high-spirited, or too something else…who knows *what* Kelly's thinking? Normally Jamie can read people pretty well, but all of a sudden it's hard to be sure of anything.

And to make matters worse, Mom is talking about the need for more responsibility around the house. Oh, fine, miss two days of chores, and you'd think the world was ending.

Doesn't Mom realize there are major distractions going on? How can she rattle on about feeding Bowser when a three-year friendship, not to mention a fortune in jewels, is at stake? Why doesn't anyone understand what it's like to have so many things to deal with all at once?

This is too much. Jamie can't handle it. Better just slam the door, grab the only CD by the only musician who understands genuine tragedy, turn up the volume and shut out the demands of the world.

Forget about Kelly. Forget about Bowser. Nobody really gets what it's like to be Jamie, anyway. Nobody stops to appreciate how difficult life can be when there are so many things going on. Nobody really cares, and that's the most heartbreaking thing of all.

Oh, but here's a knock at the door….

= = = = = = = =

Finally, the career woman who hires a detective to find the baby she gave up for adoption 13 years ago. As a Four, Anne might have had any number of reasons for the adoption – let's say she didn't feel capable of raising a child when she was only a high school sophomore, but ever since then she's tormented herself with visions of how happy she and her daughter could have been if only she hadn't made that choice.

Now she's discovered some rare disease which the adoptive parents must be warned about, and it's obvious that keeping quiet would be a terrible decision. Not only can she provide information that might save the child's life, but she can see for herself whether

her daughter suffers from feelings of abandonment. If that's the case, she doesn't know quite what she'll do…but she'll have to do something.

The detective, though, turns out to be a problem. He seems to think this search can be done by computer, and he can just mail her a report.

Anne is appalled. This is her daughter, her own flesh and blood, and how can Craig imagine she'd settle for mere words on paper?

If it would damage Emily to be confronted by her birth mother, she'll keep her distance – but surely he can see the importance of a face-to-face meeting.

Craig tries to talk her out of it, but Anne convinces him this will be best for everyone. It's sweet that he's worried about her getting hurt, and she senses that this man has some private sorrow of his own, but facing pain is the only way to get through it. In fact, maybe she can help him deal with his own troubles as well.

No sooner has he confided in her about the loss of his wife and son than they locate Emily, who's either blissfully happy with her adoptive parents or a rebellious teenager.

Either way, the drama escalates. Maybe Anne realizes that her daughter hasn't missed her at all and mourns the lost years, or maybe she sees that her beloved child is suffering "with people who don't understand what it's like to feel things deeply" and envies their ability to help. Big disaster, big turmoil.

Craig is worried about her overreacting to every possibility, and she's worried about *him* turning off all his emotions. They can't retreat behind some all-just-fine shell!

So maybe they'll decide they need each other for a new perspective on life. Or maybe they'll decide each other is the last thing they need. Maybe she'll concoct a plan to meet Emily. Or maybe he'll convince her to turn her emotional energy elsewhere, and they'll have another child together.

Keep in mind that even if Anne does turn her attention to a new life with Craig, she's still a Four. A happier, healthier Four who's overcome the fatal flaw of envy – mourning the tedium of ordinary life compared to the dramatic grandeur that *could* exist – but a Four nonetheless.

Nobody changes their type. They can change their outlook on life, they can change the traits which have kept them from being the best they can be, but their fundamental type never changes.

Because remember how all nine types can be terrific people? A happy ending just means that this particular type has found their best self. A tragic ending means they've found it and turned away. An either-way ending means they haven't found it yet...but maybe they will in the next story.

You're the writer. You can pick. And readers who share your view of the world will be delighted with whatever choice you make.

CHAPTER FIVE

QUIZ

- ☐ Are you happier by yourself than in a group?
- ☐ Do you often feel shy or ill at ease in a social situation?
- ☐ Do you dislike confrontations?
- ☐ Is privacy something you value strongly?
- ☐ Do you keep your feelings to yourself?
- ☐ Do you ever feel that you should be more generous?
- ☐ Do you view yourself as perceptive?
- ☐ Is self-reliance important to you?
- ☐ Do you prefer reading about an experience to actually doing it?
- ☐ Do you like to be alone with your interests for hours on end?

___ **TOTAL FOR FIVE**

TYPE FIVE: The Observer, The Thinker, The Analyzer

Most Fives would prefer to be behind a book than out there involved in the world.

Observation matters to them. They like to study things, analyze things, understand things – all kinds of things.

An archetypal Five might be a scientist alone in a lab, blissfully studying specimens under a microscope, and that's as accurate an image as any. But another Five might be enraptured with the study of ballet costumes, or Brahma bulls, or Scottish history, or mother-daughter relationships.

What matters is the study. The accumulation of data. Gathering enough knowledge to really understand what's what. This is the kind of understanding that might require some detachment from not only the subject under analysis, but also from the world at large.

Fives are pretty good at keeping themselves at a distance from what can seem like invasive demands. When they're involved in a project, the last thing they need is someone expecting them to drop everything and meet for lunch.

In fact, they draw their energy and inspiration not from the company of other people, but from solitude. Privacy is important to a Five. They like having their own space, whether it's physical or simply emotional.

If they're crowded in the rush-hour train station with people packed back-to-back, that won't bother them as long as they have some psychic distance. Give them a problem to analyze, or a book to read, and they don't care how many people are squeezed around them. They've got their attention occupied, and they're content.

Contentment is easy for a Five who's engrossed in a project. Picture somebody wrapped up in a book with a pad and pencil at hand, marking a paragraph and racing through pages for just the right note, aglow with the joy of discovery. For Fives, there's nothing more exhilarating.

Life is tougher when they're faced with demands from people who want their emotional involvement, who prefer hearing about their feelings rather than their thoughts. That's not where Fives are comfortable.

Studying and learning are infinitely preferable to doing and feeling. If people are divided into Mind, Body and Heart types – and, by the way, more writers tend to be Mind types – you can tell where the Fives belong.

Even when they're involved in feeling and doing as well as thinking, Fives like to keep things compartmentalized. Over here is the job. Over there is family life. Here's the museum. There's the church. Co-workers in that corner, a friend from grade school in that corner, church friends here, cousin Charlie over there. If someone suggested inviting all those people to the same party, the Five would be surprised. "Charlie doesn't know my co-workers, so what would be the point?"

(As a Five, I'm always astonished when a friend suggests I join her and another friend of hers for lunch. How can she go around mixing friendships that way? It always seems to work fine, but I have yet to suggest such a radical course of action with any of my friends!)

Friendships are fine with Fives, but what they treasure most is the life of the mind. Because that's so important to them, they don't spend a lot of time worrying about what they own.

In fact, Fives take pride in getting by without much in the way of material goods. Possessions can tie you\ down, distract you from what really matters. If the ten-year-old car runs fine, why buy a new one?

On the other hand, if the only way to understand a specific topic is to buy the $20,000 test system, Fives won't have any problem spending that money. Their reluctance to accumulate goods isn't so much about frugality as it is about the lack of attachment.

Detachment is one of a Five's strongest traits. But that doesn't necessarily keep them from being involved in the world. Fives who want to share their knowledge become wonderful teachers and writers. There's no one who can make learning more exciting than a Five.

Famous Fives

Michael Crichton exemplifies a Five who delves into subjects that intrigue him and shares what he's learned with the world. What would happen if dinosaur DNA were recovered? *Jurassic Park*. What's it like practicing medicine at a big-city hospital? *ER*. Suppose time travel were feasible. *Timeline*. Each of his books or movies or TV shows reveals a new take on some topic, whether it's science fiction or history or present-day society.

Daniel Day-Lewis, when starring in *Last Of The Mohicans*, prepared for his role by living the way a frontier scout in those times would actually live...spending weeks on end alone in the woods, taking care of his own food and shelter.

Such intense, wholehearted study is typical of the Five's passion for understanding.

Speaking of movies, that same attention to knowledge of a character shows up in the acting of Al Pacino, Michelle Pfeiffer and Ralph Fiennes. Greta Garbo, with her famous "I want to be alone" attitude, was surely a Five. And look at directors Alfred Hitchcock and George Lucas, both of whom created incredibly detailed, thoughtfully researched scenes and situations. Fives can see dimensions that other types never notice.

The same is true for artists like Georgia O'Keeffe, who retreated to the desert with her work. Or photographer Annie Liebowitz, who studies her subjects with the perceptive eye of a Five. Or authors Larry McMurtry, Ursula LeGuin and John LeCarré, who create a whole range of compelling worlds for the mind.

Good old Albert Einstein, a classic "ivory tower" professor, represents the practicality of a Five. Supposedly his wardrobe consisted of five identical shirts and five identical pairs of pants, so he never needed to waste time worrying about what to wear!

Five's Heroic Strengths

You probably know some Fives. In fact, as a writer, you're more likely to *be* a Five than if your profession were less solitary and less dependent on the life of the mind. I'd never tell a group of hockey players or cabaret performers that their number includes a lot of Fives, but it's a pretty safe statement to make to writers.

So what are a Five's biggest strengths?

The gift of detachment lets Fives be remarkably non-judgmental and accepting of people around them. They find it easy to understand their friends' perspective, even when *they* don't share it. Their curiosity about everything in the world makes them great listeners, as long as they don't feel invaded.

Because emotional entanglements can feel invasive or even overwhelming, they rarely ask for help with anything. (An exception would be asking the reference librarian for the latest journal.) They're used to coming up with answers, and relying on themselves for whatever they need.

A Five will never wake you up at three in the morning sobbing over a crisis. In fact, they rarely have a crisis that can't be dealt with by re-examining the situation from a different perspective.

New ideas will never strike Fives as threatening or dangerous. What matters is the truth, the reality...even if the reality is that people are more comfortable with fantasy. Fives have no problem with that reality, or with any other reality. Their gift is for clarity, for seeing the world as it is, for noticing patterns that other types rarely spot.

They're easily able to practice what the Buddhists call "non-attachment," because they're good at staying objective, looking at the facts when everyone else around them is focusing more on emotion. All of which can add up to a very heroic character.

Five's Fatal Flaws

On the other hand, if you want your Five character to face some problems, detachment can be taken too far. Picture an ivory-tower professor who refuses to acknowledge that Junior needs a hug.

Fives can get so wrapped up in their study that they withdraw from the world altogether. If the character is a contemplative monk, there's no problem. But if someone needs emotional interaction and the Five never even notices, there'll be some conflict.

The conflict can be even worse if the Five *does* notice, but feels incapable of providing any involvement. You can see how this will create problems not only for the person who's emotionally hungry, but also for the Five.

If every type has a "deadly sin," Five's is avarice. Their greed isn't for jewels or fame, but for privacy and knowledge. (Whenever I emerge from the library with a stack of books, I feel like a pirate king glorying in chests of gold.) Fives can hoard their privacy and knowledge the same as a miser hoards money.

So the only way for them to overcome their fatal flaw is by opening up to the world and learning to share.

Their greatest growth and achievement comes from letting other people in, from sharing their knowledge and even their feelings, from letting their detachment relax just enough to allow some genuine emotion.

This kind of change can be a dramatic turnaround for a Five. Imagine a scientist who spends every day holed up in the lab, learning that orphaned nephew Junior is lonely. The scientist will apply reason to the problem, hire a babysitter, research what five-year-olds need for healthy bones, but still resist actually hugging the kid until the happy ending. Talk about a classic triumph!

Fives As Children

Look around a school playground at recess, and it's easy to spot the young Fives. They're the ones sitting on the steps reading a library book with fascinated attention rather than playing with the other kids.

They have no problem entertaining themselves, and can be perfectly happy spending hours alone with books, collections, models, games or any other solitary activity. In fact, if they're urged to join the neighbor kids for Hide & Seek, they can feel resentful or uncomfortable or impatient…why would they want to do *this*?

But even so, some small part of them wants to be included. Even though they're more comfortable alone, once in a while they like to be involved with other people.

On those occasions, a Five child will be happier interacting with one or two close friends than with a whole gang of friends. Time spent one-on-one is preferable to time spent in a group, where so many emotions and expectations are flying every which way. With one friend at a time, Fives can feel more in control of the emotional input.

In a society that tends to value outgoing, demonstrative behavior, the Five might feel abnormal. But during the time they spend alone, they're building tremendous self-reliance and strength.

This makes it easier for them to withstand peer pressure as they enter adolescence, because they've spent a lifetime developing the habit of thinking for themselves.

It's no surprise that young Fives, just like adult Fives, are highly observant of whatever catches their interest. If it doesn't interest them, it doesn't register. They can't likely tell you their teacher's favorite color, but if you ask what the teacher said about the light refractions of a rainbow, they can impress you by bringing the subject to life.

Fives At Work

Fives' remarkable skill at observation comes in handy on the job. If they're working in any area that requires clear perception, clear thought and a love of study, they're going to feel right at home.

On the other hand, the worst imaginable job for a Five would involve spending every moment actively sharing emotions with strangers, never having time alone to think, and never being able to focus on a particular area of interest.

But Fives who have some autonomy to pursue knowledge in any area are going to be a tremendous asset on the job.

Whether or not they've developed strong social skills, they've definitely developed the skills to sustain concentration over a long period of time...and to study a problem from every conceivable angle.

They also embody the advantages of integrity and calm. Because emotions don't get in their way, they can be towers of strength and reason during a crisis situation. And because the approval or appreciation of their peers doesn't matter as much to a Five as to a more sociable type, they're not likely to get involved in office politics. Their goal is accuracy, their passion is knowledge.

To a Five, knowledge is power. Facts are more trustworthy than feelings. A meeting which segues from job-related discussion to a chat about how people spent the weekend will have Fives writhing in their chairs, wishing the talk would get back to the topic at hand. Social chitchat is fine if that's on the agenda – they can get along if they have to – but it's never their first choice for the ideal way to spend an afternoon.

Autonomy is a treasure. So a Five who's in charge of some specific area, and who's given the flexibility to get the job done, will pursue that mission with remarkable success.

Fives In Relationships

If you've ever heard someone say, "Sure, I'm happy with Pat, but if we split up tomorrow it wouldn't be the end of the world," it's possible that the person doesn't care about Pat all that much.

Or it's possible that the person cares deeply, and is a Five.

Fives have a hard time acknowledging that they need someone. They're far more comfortable not needing anyone, knowing that they can be fine on their own. This makes commitment scary, and even a long-married Five might still say periodically that Pat isn't all that necessary to a happy life…because in fact Pat *is*, and they're afraid to acknowledge that.

Since Fives tend to compartmentalize their lives, relationships are scattered in various areas. No one person gets their entire attention, their entire spirit, their entire self. This lets them maintain the privacy they crave, and anyone close to a Five will recognize the value of allowing some distance.

When Fives aren't feeling crowded, they can be wonderfully open and free. But if they're pressed to share their emotions, or to share anything beyond factual data, they back away. On the surface they might still be engaged in conversation, but in reality they're just going through the motions. Their heart isn't all there.

This detachment makes a Five the ideal friend to confide in. They respect confidences more than any other type, and wouldn't dream of sharing someone's secret without a specific okay. Secrets are powerful, and Fives have a deep respect for privacy.

In fact, one way Fives will offer friendship is by sharing some private knowledge, like a new discovery or a secret code. "Sharing confidences" with someone they trust is a major step toward a solid relationship…one in which they can feel both autonomous and close.

Five's Individual Subtype

"My home is my castle," says this Five. Home is the best place for preserving a sense of self, and it can be arranged in whatever way will best suit someone who favors a life of the mind. If home is shared with other people, the Five is likely to have a private space – somewhere to retreat, to be completely alone. Even if it's just an armchair with a good reading lamp, that armchair is truly a castle.

Fives who value self-preservation find it easy to keep life simple. They're not about to get dragged down with bags full of goods, or even with too many people who make demands on their time and energy and privacy. What keeps their spirits intact is the ability to let go, to avoid getting sucked into big emotions or spontaneous outbursts or other people's plans.

Fives are almost always self-reliant, and these Fives are even more so. They don't like owing money, owing favors, owing attention. They don't like having to report to anyone. They like to go their own way, staying clear of involvement with anyone or anything they haven't deliberately sought out for themselves.

Because they treasure their independence, they'll do whatever it takes to preserve it. Their time is precious. Their privacy is precious. Their freedom is precious. And self-preservation means guarding those treasures in whatever castle they can create for themselves.

Five's Intimacy Subtype

Fives love knowledge. A close knowledge of someone else can be exhilarating. And a Five who embodies the relational subtype loves the intimacy of sharing knowledge with someone else.

It could be a lover, or a co-worker, or a friend. What matters is that the relationship between these two people involves a shared awareness. Victorians used to say that couples who were on the verge of announcing their engagement "shared an understanding," and Fives appreciate that more deeply than any other type.

To a Five, the greatest intimacy comes from sharing an understanding. It might involve sharing childhood dreams, or sexual fantasies, or secret embarrassments. Or it might involve sharing research notes, or a working outline, or a new hypothesis.

Fives value people who respect their boundaries, and that means not offering or seeking any more information – personal or professional – than the Five feels comfortable sharing.

Because Fives value privacy so deeply, any secrets shared with a Five will never be revealed on the five o'clock news. They respect other people's privacy as much as their own, and view any unauthorized disclosure as an unforgivable betrayal. But with people they trust, the relational Fives are surprisingly good at sharing confidences...and never, ever divulging them.

Five's Social Subtype

A Five who appreciates being part of the group will never relinquish that most precious commodity, autonomy. However, it's possible for a Five to be a vital, contributing member of the group while still preserving innate privacy – and for the group to never even suspect there's anything hidden beneath the social surface.

With their passion for knowledge, Fives enjoy mixing and mingling with other people in their fields of study. They'll happily attend gatherings to seek out new information or to meet experts who might shed new light on subjects that interest them. A truly social Five will even join the gang for dinner after the meeting, and enjoy chatting with the entire group.

However, they'll still have their intellectual hat on even during the most sociable Happy Hour. Let someone in the group ask a question, and the Five will happily swing into a lecture. A socially minded Five can make the lecture entertaining enough to keep the group happy, and still share whatever treasured knowledge is called for.

Being part of the "in" crowd, for a Five, doesn't mean hanging out with the most popular people – but rather with the most knowledgeable people.

Any society has its experts, and Fives love being in that elite circle. Sharing their own expertise is their way of contributing to the good of the entire group...or the entire society around them.

Fives With Other Types

Fives can get along with other types just fine, but that doesn't provide much conflict for an author. Instead, take a look at what can go wrong when a Five encounters any of the nine types.

Five & One

Five wants to focus on the current research; One wants to focus on getting things done *right* – too bad if that means interrupting Five. Five shuts the door. One takes offense. Five opens it and sighs. One blows up.

Five & Two

Five is wrapped up in solitude when Two asks, "Would you like a sandwich?" "No, I'm busy." "But you need nourishment." "No, thanks." "But I want to take care of you." "I don't need it!" "What, you don't need *me*?"

Five & Three

Time for Three's inauguration as new mayor; Five shows up late because things got busy in the lab. Three demands, "Don't you appreciate the importance of my work?" Five retorts, "Don't you appreciate the importance of *mine*?"

Five & Four

Four is getting upset about a crisis with a friend; Five is detached. Four asks, "Don't you *care* about people?" "Sure, but you're being too dramatic." "You're being too aloof – you've never cared about me *or* my feelings!"

Five & Five

He's finished his project. She's just now starting hers. He wouldn't mind a little celebration, but she's busy. He should understand that. It's just, well…he misses her. How can he feel that way? Stupid, yeah, but…

Five & Six

The lightning-bolt experiment is almost ready; does Six want to watch? "No, wait, this could kill someone!" "Probably not, and in any case it's for a good cause." "Nothing's worth a risk like that." "Not even my life's work?"

Five & Seven

"Oh, boy," says Seven, "a party!" "No, thanks, you go." "Come on, it'll be fun!" "I'd rather stay home and read." "Don't you want to be with me?" "At a *party*?" "We never have any fun." "We have great privacy." "What about our *life*?"

Five & Eight

"Okay, Five, you need to pick up the delivery by six." "I'll try and remember." "You won't remember unless I remind you, right?" "Well, you're so good at organizing things…" "But why can't I ever count on you for backup?"

Five & Nine

"Hey, Nine, listen to this great research proposal." "Oh, my show's on – but okay, go ahead." "No, if you'd rather watch your show, I guess that's more important." "I said, go ahead!" "Never mind, you'll resent every minute of it."

You see how none of these is a life-and-death conflict? (Well, except maybe the lightning bolt.) But each one can be intensified or relieved, depending on where you are in the story.

Some conflicts may strike you as overly dramatic or overly boring. That's okay. That's a clear sign that your story doesn't *need* such a conflict. You may have enough conflict already. If you do need more, though, it's a safe bet that at least one of these examples will spark some ideas. And that's where the fun begins.

Scenarios With Fives

No matter what kind of story you're telling, the characters' personality types will make a difference in the conflict that arises. Here are examples of five stories – about a detective, a princess, a cowboy, a teenager and a career woman – where the protagonist will come into conflict because of his or her enneagram type.

= = = = = = = =

Let's start with the cop trying to track down a blackmailer who's threatening the arrogant father-in-law of his beloved daughter. Jack Warner is a Five.

So of course he's going to pursue this new quest with all the brain-power he's got. Even though he find Karen's father-in-law insufferably arrogant (maybe the guy is another Five who always knows better trivia at Karen's family brunches), he has his mission. Maybe he's doing it as a favor to his daughter or maybe as part of the job, where Jack excels at assignments that let him rely on his own intelligence to track down blackmailers.

Either way, he'll bring to this assignment his usual keen wit and tremendous skill at following a paper trail. He's willing to put in all the time and energy it takes to solve this problem, and he feels confident in his ability to come up with the right answer. If he deals with underworld informants, they've come to trust his promises of confidentiality. There's never been a problem he can't solve when he puts his mind to it.

But something's different this time. It almost seems as if the blackmailer is as skilled at evasion as Jack is at sleuthing. Even worse, Jack's new assistant believes in personal chat between every computer printout, and he's distracted by his frustration at not being able to focus on the numbers.

Or maybe a fellow cop offers him a tip – if he beats up on some street-corner thug, the punk will reveal the blackmailer's identity – and Jack refuses to take that route when he knows his brain is better than the criminal's.

Maybe he gets so wrapped up in studying the blackmailer's notes that he forgets to go home one night. Maybe his wife is hurt, although you'd think she'd be used to all-nighters if they've been together long enough to have a married daughter. Maybe the lack of sleep causes him to miss some obvious clue, and he's appalled at himself.

In terms of overcoming his fatal flaw – which is greed for privacy – Jack may have to give up his lone-ranger style of work and accept help from the other cop. He may have to admit he can't outwit this blackmailer alone. He may have to admit to his daughter that his skill isn't everything he thought it would be...and she'll either turn away in disgust or assure him that she loves him for trying.

It all depends on how you want to handle the story.

= = = = = = = =

Next comes the princess trying to choose the best ally to defend her kingdom from an invasion of trolls – either the renegade dragon-rider, or the vampire lord.

As a Five, Aliana will approach this situation logically. She'll determine the pros and cons of each possibility. What will Varek demand in exchange for his help? Can she figure out some way to refuse him blood from every peasant in the keep?

Is Kelwyn someone she can trust? If she joins forces with the dragon-slayer, how fully will he expect to share in her private life?

She might dither over the potential outcomes of every action until the trolls are advancing on the castle, but now she has to make a decision. Given that her mission is to save the kingdom, will she be better off sacrificing the blood of peasants (who'd likely be killed by trolls in any case) or her treasured solitude?

Well, she's a princess and she's memorized the code of ethics. So she'll cast her lot with the dragon-slayer, but she's smart enough to keep the vampire lord on call. If Kelwyn can't defeat the trolls by sundown, she'll backtrack and accept Varek's offer of an alliance instead.

But now the peasants are horrified at the very idea of a blood sacrifice. Aliana's getting frustrated – she didn't ask for this responsibility in the first place, and no matter how carefully she evaluates her options, somebody's going to think she's stupid. All she's got is her ability to think and figure things out, and right now it doesn't seem to be enough!

Things are looking pretty grim, here. Of course she wants the kingdom to be safe, but she also wants the satisfaction of achieving that safety through her own intelligent skill. She certainly doesn't want to share decision making with either the dragon-slayer or the vampire lord, and yet neither of them seems willing to accept her decisions regarding the most logical way to proceed.

Maybe she'll overcome her desire to come up with the best plan for every conceivable situation in time to choose a course of action. Maybe it'll fail.

Or maybe she'll hold out for what she perceives as the soundest solution, convinced that she's got better insights than anyone else, long after the trolls have defeated the dragon-slayer and the vampire lord has started lining up peasants. Maybe she'll rally at the last minute and decide that while logic is important, so are cooperation and action, and thereby save the day.

Once again, it all depends on how you want to handle the story!

= = = = = = = =

Now, here's our cowboy facing off against the cattle rustlers. Buck is a Five, and as such he's perfectly content living in a solitary bunkhouse and watching the cows all night. Only problem is, rustlers are picking off the ranch's cattle two and three at a time, and that means he's got to take action.

Action isn't Buck's strong point. Thinking is. He suspects that keeping watch all night with a loaded shotgun might be all it takes to save the day, but he can't help wishing there were some cleaner, more precise solution than that.

Well, maybe he can came up with some clever plan to divert the herd from their usual run. He might spend quite a bit of time charting the flow of the creek and figuring out which way the steers are likely to bolt if he fires three shots during a dust storm. He might invent a whole new way of protecting cattle from wildfire while he's at it, but this still isn't stopping the rustlers.

Okay, now it's getting personal. Buck knows he shouldn't take it personally – this is an academic problem, one he can surely solve if he identifies the right approach – but it's downright annoying that he can't seem to outwit these low-lifes who probably can't even write their names. (Even though Buck never spent more than six months in a one-room schoolhouse on the prairie, you can bet he taught himself to read from the family Bible or a dog-eared copy of Shakespeare and has been devouring every newspaper he can get his hands on for the past ten years.)

So why can't he get the better of these rustlers? Maybe he does give in and tries the simplest approach of staying up all night with a shotgun, but something goes wrong. He gets distracted by the arc of a falling star, wondering why constellations look different in summer and winter. Or the rustlers gang up on him and leave him for dead.

Now it's really personal. Asking for help is out of the question – Buck takes pride in handling problems on his own, and his passion for autonomy means he'll refuse to accept the idea of needing backup – but it seems like acting alone isn't working as well as it has before.

Maybe the town schoolmarm was right when she said he was "too solitary." Maybe the chatty deputy had a point when he mentioned that "folks like to help their neighbors once they know 'em." Or maybe that's all just foolishness, and if he thinks hard enough he'll come up with some brilliant solution he can implement on his own.

Your story. Your cowboy. Your call.

= = = = = = = =

Let's take a look at the teenager whose only friend finds a buried treasure in the family's backyard.

Jamie is a loner, and always has been. It's hard to say exactly how this friendship with Kelly even got started, except Kelly lives nearby and doesn't seem to get that Jamie doesn't really *need* any companionship. And it's not like there's anything wrong with being friends – in fact, Jamie would probably miss hanging out together if the family moved away – but now Kelly has come up with something kind of strange.

No telling how that cache of emeralds wound up in the back yard, but Jamie senses that asking questions would be a mistake. Better to research this independently than go talking to the police, or even Mom and Dad. There might be some robbery-murder on the books, and if so it's just a matter of handing over the evidence, but suppose there's no record of any stolen emeralds?

Kelly is clamoring to announce their discovery, but Jamie doesn't want to leap into anything. Getting all the facts first is always the best way to go, and they can check news stories for the past 115 years if necessary. Matter of fact, it'd be a good idea to investigate how much dirt clung to the jewels – that might help narrow down the decade they were buried.

It's hard to concentrate on research, though, with Kelly insisting "finders keepers" and planning what they can do with either the reward money or the sale of unclaimed emeralds. Jamie has a lot to juggle, trying to keep Kelly quiet until they've gathered more facts, and figuring out the best way to break the news to Mom and Dad once the facts are lined up.

They'll be upset they didn't hear the news right away – they always want more of Jamie's life than they have any right to – and it's a pretty sure bet that they'll launch into another one of those "why don't you ever open up?" sessions.

Kelly, though, announces that the facts aren't as important as staking a claim on what they've found. In fact, Kelly is going to phone the city lost-and-found tomorrow, and says they might as well start figuring out how to spend the reward money.

But the reward money is academic. Sure, Jamie can set it aside for college, although winning a scholarship seems pretty certain, but who cares about money when there's a mystery staring them right in the face? Doesn't Kelly understand the importance of figuring this out?

Maybe Kelly will give in. Or maybe not. Maybe Jamie will be forced to change. Or maybe not. It's your story!

= = = = = = = =

Finally, the career woman who hires a detective to find the baby she gave up for adoption 13 years ago. As a Five, Anne might have had any number of reasons for the adoption – let's say she didn't feel capable of raising a child at the time, because she's always had trouble getting close to people. The last thing an innocent baby needs is a mother who prefers books to relationships.

But now she's discovered some rare disease which the adoptive parents must be warned about, and she can't help admitting she's curious to see the child she gave birth to. Not to interfere with Emily's life – she researched the parents so thoroughly that she knows her daughter is better off with them. Still, curiosity is only normal. Only human. Isn't it?

What she hasn't expected is the kind of caring attention her detective shows at every turn. Craig is different from anyone she's ever met, and part of her wants to let this relationship unfold…just to see where it leads.

But the more rational part knows that's foolish. Sure, maybe Craig likes her right now – maybe he really *is* attracted to women who value brains above beauty – but that can't possibly last. Even if he means it, she'll disappoint him in the end.

She's never mastered the art of intimacy, the sharing of souls that most lovers seem to take for granted, and she can't expect Craig to put up with her just-the-facts personality for long.

Maybe she should hire another detective, except this one's so skilled at his work. Maybe she should show up for their dinner date in her most dowdy clothes to prove she's not the woman he wants. Or maybe she should listen when he insists there's more passion below her calm surface than she's ever been willing to acknowledge.

This can become even more complicated when he completes the mission of finding Emily. Maybe she's overwhelmed by the rush of love she feels for this child.

Or maybe she's convinced that, having deliberately given up any chance for a mother-daughter relationship, she can't possibly expect to succeed at any other.

Maybe she sees in Emily the same kind of person she's always seen in herself, and comes to appreciate those solitary qualities. Maybe she realizes she wants something more from life, and here's her chance. Maybe she sees no resemblance at all, and feels glad about it for Emily's sake...or sorry that her daughter will never know the kind of satisfaction Anne has known, which makes her appreciate who she is.

Maybe that convinces her to open her heart with Craig. Or maybe not.

It's all up to you.

Keep in mind that even if she does opt to trade her solitary life for a life with Craig, she's still a Five. A happier, healthier Five who's overcome the fatal flaw of avarice – greed for privacy and solitude and personal space – but a Five nonetheless.

Nobody changes their type. They can change their outlook on life, they can change the traits which have kept them from being the best they can be, but their fundamental type never changes.

Because remember how all nine types can be terrific people? A happy ending just means that this particular type has found their best self. A tragic ending means they've found it and turned away. An either-way ending means they haven't found it yet...but maybe they will in the next story.

You're the writer. You can pick. And readers who share your view of the world will be delighted with whatever choice you make.

CHAPTER SIX

QUIZ

- ☐ Do you stick up for the underdog?
- ☐ Do you tend to focus on worst-case scenarios?
- ☐ Are you more aware of your surroundings than others are?
- ☐ Do you find it hard to trust?
- ☐ Is it often hard for you to make a decision?
- ☐ Do you generally take a cautious approach to life?
- ☐ Do people often say you're a good worker?
- ☐ Are you wary of compliments?
- ☐ Do you tend to be stubborn?
- ☐ Is loyalty very important to you?

___ **TOTAL FOR SIX**

TYPE SIX: The Trooper, The Questioner, The Loyal Skeptic

Just about everyone is concerned with security in some form or another, but Sixes take the prize. Security is their primary focus, and it's a round-the-clock job.

There's nobody better at spotting potential risks and figuring out ways to cope. If you're having dinner with Sixes at some brand new restaurant, you can be sure they've already determined where to find the emergency exit. If you hear a strange noise outside, the Six is more likely to assume it's a burglar than to assume it's a stray cat. If you're starting a new project, you can count on Six to identify all the potential loopholes.

Such constant vigilance takes a toll, though, and Sixes deal with their anxiety in many different ways.

They might seek protection wherever they can find it, they might develop a fabulous sense of humor to get them through scary situations, or they might resolutely square off against any and every possible danger.

If there's no particular danger within view, that still doesn't matter – Sixes know the biggest risks are those you can't see.

This makes them exceptionally good at reading other people's motives. They're skilled at analyzing a conversation or situation that wouldn't make much impression on other types, and determining exactly what Aunt Mary *meant* when she said, "Good morning." They don't take anything at face value. They're always willing to ask questions, because knowing the full story means security.

Even with their strong troubleshooting skills, Sixes are often plagued by doubts. And their response may be fight or flight…or sometimes a mixture. If they're at a sports event surrounded by angry fans whose team is losing, they might start by retreating to another row of seats and whistling nonchalantly all the while. But then they might realize that whistling could make them a target, and feel even more vulnerable. So they'll face off against the nearest person and demand, "What are *you* looking at?"

Or they might start out by confronting the rioters and sending them scattering. But then, realizing that they may have overreacted, they'll feel even more anxious. So they'll turn to the nearest safe-looking person and suggest, "Let's find someplace more quiet. Walk with me?"

This constant back-and-forth rhythm takes a lot of energy, and Sixes are skilled at juggling a lot of balls at once.

When everything around them seems perfectly secure, they feel uneasy – life is too good to be true.

But when faced with an earthquake or a gang of terrorists, they come into their own. They've spent a lifetime training for the worst possible disasters, and now that disaster has arrived, Sixes handle it with consummate bravery.

Such steady vigilance makes them very responsible and hardworking, and Sixes often wish there were some rule book to cover every situation imaginable. Even without any rule book, they're strongly committed to those they care about…and always aware of potential risks. Sixes treasure the repeated reassurance that they're safe and loved and cared for, because they're used to doubting *everything*.

Including authority. Sixes are always aware of authority, wanting to make sure the police are doing their job and the doctors are diagnosing correctly and God's people are protecting their own. They'll gladly place their trust in a power they believe in, but first they want proof.

If they ever suspect some authority isn't living up to expectations, they won't hesitate to stage a confrontation. Sure, that might be scary, but living with doubts is even scarier. If leading a revolution is what it takes to feel secure, a Six will be the first one out of the trenches.

Whatever it takes to ensure safety, Sixes will gladly embrace. Sometimes that means aggressively rebelling. Sometimes it means carefully seeking approval. Sometimes it means using tremendous charm, wit and intelligence to gather a community of people who can be counted on. And making sure someone knows where to find the exit…

Famous Sixes

"What do women want?" If ever a question showed the desire for security in an unknown realm, it's that one by Sigmund Freud. Still, not every Six displays such a yearning for security. Sometimes it's easier to spot how they've devoted their drive for security to becoming a likable person, like Mary Tyler Moore or Meg Ryan or Bob Newhart. Good, decent people…who might worry just a little more than most.

Woody Allen typifies the extreme side of worrying about danger. On the other end, Mel Gibson typifies the extreme side of confronting danger.

Most famous Sixes, at least in the movies, fall somewhere between Gene Wilder and Warren Beatty along that continuum. But you can still see the quest for global or personal security in actors like Dustin Hoffman and Gene Hackman, Paul Newman and Robert Redford, Julia Roberts and Sally Field and Marilyn Monroe.

You can also see it in comedians like Ellen DeGeneres, George Carlin and Jay Leno. Sixes don't mind poking fun at themselves or the world around them, as long as it'll make things better – and hopefully safer – in the long run.

That's what motivates directors like Spike Lee and Michael Moore, as well as TV personalities such as David Letterman and Phil Donahue.

And it's even more apparent in political figures like Richard Nixon, J. Edgar Hoover and George Bush.

Whether or not people agree with their methods for guaranteeing security, each one typifies the need for ensuring that the world is a safe place to be…and doing whatever it takes to make sure that'll happen.

Six's Heroic Strengths

More than any other type, Sixes value their community. When they're with their family, their friends, their co-workers, fellow church members, people from their own neighborhood, or whatever community lets them feel safe, they can afford to relax.

This makes Sixes the kind of people you want in your group. Such wholehearted loyalty is hard to find, and these people are wonderfully steady as companions, providers and friends. They'll do anything for those they love, and not even consider it a sacrifice.

Their constant awareness of possible dangers give Sixes some other heroic traits, as well. Because they know people are safer when they're liked by those around them, they often show only their most likable facets. Because laughter helps chase away fear, they often develop a fine wit and a subtle sense of humor. Because they know what it's like to be worried, they show extra compassion for the underdog. And their ability to look past the surface gives them a creative originality you may not find in other types.

It's hard to put anything over on a Six. But when a Six cares about you, you know your flaws have been spotted and dismissed. The Six loves you anyway, and once you're considered "just like family" or "one of our own," you're assured of someone on your side no matter how tough things might get.

If things *do* get tough, Sixes make great troubleshooters, and their courage under fire can be truly impressive.

Whether they rebel against untrustworthy authorities or seek to understand every nuance of trustworthy authorities, Sixes are great at recognizing loopholes…then finding ways to make the system work for them, *and* for the community they hold dear.

Six's Fatal Flaws

Fear is a pretty constant factor in the life of a Six. Whether they're doggedly challenging every situation that might raise a ripple of concern, or throwing all of their loyalty toward some institution they've judged safe enough to believe in, they know what it's like to live with fear.

This can make them evasive, overly cautious, or reluctant to trust. Sixes may have a hard time making up their mind, because ambivalence might feel safer than action. When that happens, they'll find it easy to procrastinate, and repeated failure to take action may erode their self-confidence to the point where they feel even more vulnerable.

The classic images would be either a timid weakling who skulks in corners "just following orders" and hoping to stay out of trouble, *or* a thundering aggressor who's determined to bite the dog first. Either way, the Six is driven by fear.

And non-stop worry can become so tiring that they may try the other extreme instead, setting up a boing-boing bounce. The former bully will make it a point to keep a low profile, while the former sulker will burst into a raging tirade.

Two sides of the same coin, right? The most well-adjusted Sixes recognize that, and let both sides spill over onto each other. When they feel uneasy, they don't automatically go into a fight or flight mode – instead they remember the importance of having faith in themselves.

But until that happens, your Six characters can come up against some wonderful conflicts. Whether they start by cowering or rebelling, by seeking protection or threatening anyone who doesn't follow their line, there's plenty of room for growth and change while Sixes gradually learn to accept the uncertainties of life and trust that things can always be worked out.

Sixes As Children

Any child who wants to know "who's in charge" is very likely a Six. Just like their adult counterparts, little Sixes are always aware of authority and always more secure when they know exactly what's going to happen.

Known quantities are appealing, and these children feel much better when they're in control of their environment. If that means being extra charming or extra bossy, fine – they'll do whatever it takes. They might become exceptionally good at defending themselves with humor or with anger. No matter how strong their defenses, though, they're always on the lookout for danger.

Questioning things makes them feel safer. They want to know what the grownups – parents, teachers and anyone else in charge – are thinking. Maybe they'll go along with it in hopes of ensuring their own safety, or maybe they'll rebel against it in hopes of proving they're not afraid.

Even as children, Sixes can bounce from fight to flight and back again with remarkable speed.

Sometimes they'll have trouble making a decision, because they can see all the potential outcomes so clearly. The lucky little Sixes are those whose parents show confidence in their child's ability to deal with new situations, because that can give them the courage to try something unknown.

A young Six might spend more time worrying than other kids in the class, and panicking over small things isn't unheard of. Having clear limits and a definite structure helps them, even when they're showing the rebellious side of their personality.

Whether they're acting shy and fearful or aggressive and fearless, they're driven by the quest for security. These children care deeply about ensuring safety for themselves, *and* for those who've earned their fierce loyalty.

Sixes At Work

It's no surprise that Sixes, who believe in loyalty and responsibility, are known for being hard workers. They'll support the team through thick and thin, and are especially well suited to working in the military, academia or the justice system – places with clear rules and solid structure.

A Six may become so loyal to the job that any personal freedom is cheerfully traded for the promise of security. "The company needs me to work around the clock for five years in a row? No problem."

However, there's also the possibility of rebellion. "They've been treating me like a slave for four years. I'm going to take over the company headquarters and show 'em they can't get away with this!" Such a Six can be transformed from a devoted employee to an impassioned attacker.

Either way, Sixes will place more emphasis on the power of authority than any other type. Whether they view the boss as benevolent or malevolent, they almost always credit the person in charge with more power than actually exists.

Sixes who are satisfied with their work are wonderfully discreet and diplomatic, good at avoiding hurt feelings and seeking out win-win solutions. They have strong analytical powers, and will frequently spot potential problems nobody else has seen.

When a worst-case scenario arises, they no longer have to deal with doubts and can turn all their attention to trouble shooting. At such times, when they're focused on action rather than worry, they perform at their absolute best.

But if this brilliant Six is honored as Employee Of The Year, the anxiety will return with even greater force. High visibility means high vulnerability, so a quiet bonus is far preferable to a seat in the limelight...where you can't quite tell who's watching you.

Sixes In Relationships

A Six might not mind hearing, "Hey, you look fabulous." An even better compliment, though, is, "You have a smudge on your shoe, but otherwise you look fabulous." For these perennial doubters, a spoonful of medicine makes the sugar go down far more believably.

Because Sixes are very cautious about letting down their guard, they want to continue making sure their relationships are working. Even if they've known you for ten years with never a harsh word, there's no such thing as too much reassurance.

And specific reassurance is better than general: "Sweetie, I've loved you every day of the past ten years we've been married and

I've never regretted my commitment to you, except when you forgot to buy milk last Wednesday, but now I'm over that and I still love you more than anyone."

Until they relax enough to trust that they're not going to be abandoned or taken advantage of, Sixes will hold back from acknowledging how much someone means to them.

It's safer not to risk disappointment, so instead they'll try to stay ambivalent. Naturally, they assume that everyone feels the same way about *them* – "why should anyone stick their neck out just to be with me?" – which can leave them defensive and hurting when they meet the mate of their dreams.

The mate of their dreams will be someone who knows how to provide constant reassurance. Who appreciates that occasional bouts of sarcasm or withdrawal come from fear rather than from anything wrong with the relationship. Who encourages the Six to focus on not just the worst possible outcome, but also on the best. And who consistently tells the truth, making Sixes feel confident that, even with a smudged shoe, they really *do* look fabulous.

Six's Individual Subtype

Sixes who look for self-preservation look first to their friends. While most types who seek individual security tend to find it within themselves, Sixes feel most safe when they're with people they can count on.

That means people who know them thoroughly, which means the ability to relax and stop worrying about making the right impression.

So this individual-subtype Six will do whatever it takes to keep friends close. Those friends will probably view the Six as unusually warm and genial, maybe even ingratiating, and someone who can always be relied on for complete and utter loyalty. Of course, such loyalty is expected in return…and it's easy to give, because the Six is careful to use all the self-deprecating humor and charm needed to keep a circle of friends nearby.

Being liked means being protected, right? And protection is important.

That's why it makes sense to stay in the good graces of whoever might be in authority. To analyze every possible action in search of the safest possible option. To be surrounded by people who like you enough to go to bat for you.

Such people are essential to Sixes who value self-preservation. Around these friends, they know what to expect. They can occasionally let down their guard. They feel secure among people whose loyalty can be taken for granted, and they'll give their own dogged, wholehearted loyalty in return.

Six's Intimacy Subtype

When relationships are a priority, Sixes know how to make them as secure as possible. A show of strength is always good. After all, people flock to be around those whom they perceive as strong, right? And being attractive is good, too…that attracts others as well.

So a Six who values close relationships is likely to spend quite a bit of effort on appearing strong or attractive or both. This hides any fear inside.

Showing fear is a bad idea, because who could look up to somebody timid? Being looked up to and respected is far safer.

And in fact, once that happens, the Six will rise to the occasion. Maybe there's still some fear underneath, but it'll never show.

Since the world is full of potential dangers, though, it makes sense to have a strong defense system. Power is good. The kind of attractiveness that makes other people leap to your defense is good. A relational Six might study martial arts or the most flattering colors, whatever's likely to pay off in terms of security.

The worst scenario would be isolation from others, because then there's no security. As long as someone is nearby to offer admiration or even to seek protection, the Six isn't alone. And that's a wonderful way to ensure the goal of safety.

Six's Societal Subtype

A Six who feels best when immersed in some group or society will be fiercely loyal to that group. Maybe even a little skeptical of outsiders – who knows, they might not have the group's best interests at heart – and certain that security is found within this society.

When making a decision, the social-subtype Six will often consult with a committee. It might be an imaginary committee, but even so, it's comprised of group members who know what's what. After all, safety depends not on the Six's individual efforts, but on the group as a whole.

Such a group is lucky to have this Six, because they're assured of a tireless worker who's devoted to the family or the company or the church or the political party or whatever unites their society. The Six might very well idealize the group's president or matriarch or general or whoever's in charge...and as long as this leader stays trustworthy, Six won't hesitate to meet any request. No sacrifice is too great if it ensures the well-being of the group.

But if the leader fails to prove trustworthy, the Six who used to carefully follow every rule will be just as quick to break every rule.

Once disillusionment sets in, there's no turning back. This Six will turn every bit of heartfelt devotion to the cause of restoring the group's well-being, no matter what that might be.

Sixes With Other Types

Sixes are great at building loyal friendships and protecting their loved ones, but that doesn't provide much conflict for an author. Instead, take a look at what can go wrong when a Six encounters any of the nine types.

Six & One

One's upset about something, but doesn't like to gripe. Six is aware of One fuming, and starts to worry. "Did I do something wrong?" "No, everything's fine." "But you're clenching your teeth." "I am *not!*" "Uh-oh, what did I *do*?"

Six & Two

Since Six is always analyzing motives, Two's usual style of nurturing might arouse some suspicion. "You're not buttering my toast because you care about me; it's only so I'll need you." "I'm just trying to be helpful." "No, there's more to it than that."

Six & Three

"This," says Three, "is the greatest plan ever." Six asks, "What about this detail?" "Aw, don't worry about it." "But something could go wrong." "Come on, you're not looking at the big picture!" "You're not looking at the details."

Six & Four

Four is excited about a new movie, but Six isn't: "I'm not so sure." "Oh, come on, take a risk." "Not all of us enjoy living on the edge." "But you need a little more drama in your life." "You've got more than enough drama for both of us."

Six & Five

Five's lightning-bolt experiment is almost ready; does Six want to watch? "No, wait, this could kill someone!" "Probably not, and in any case it's for a good cause." "Nothing's worth a risk like that." "Not even my life's work?"

Six & Six

Neither one is quite sure what to do next. Things could go wrong so easily. Why take a risk? But standing still might make things even worse. They'll feed each other's doubts, and sensing each other's fear will make them even more anxious.

Six & Seven

"It might rain," Six frets. "So, it'll be fun to get wet. You worry too much." "You don't worry enough." "I'm just trying to keep things fun." "Oh, you're saying I'm a party-pooper?" "Why do you always have to look at the dark side?"

Six & Eight

While Six considers every possible danger, Eight prefers rushing into action against any perceived opposition. "But you haven't thought this through!" "If I waited for you to analyze every single risk, we'd still be sitting here next year."

Six & Nine

They're both slow to action. "You talk first," says Six. "No, *you* go first." "I need to think about it." "No rush," says Nine, leaning back more comfortably. "Aren't you giving any thought to what *could* happen?" "Nope. Here, you go first."

You see how none of these is a life-and-death conflict? But each one can be intensified or relieved, depending on where you are in the story.

Some conflicts may strike you as overly dramatic or overly boring. That's okay. That's a clear sign that your story doesn't *need* such a conflict. You may have enough conflict already. If you do need more, though, it's a safe bet that at least one of these examples will spark some ideas. And that's where the fun begins.

Scenarios With Sixes

No matter what kind of story you're telling, the characters' personality types will make a difference in the conflict that arises. Here are examples of five stories – about a detective, a princess, a cowboy, a teenager and a career woman – where the protagonist will come into conflict because of his or her enneagram type.

= = = = = = = =

Let's start with the cop trying to track down a blackmailer who's threatening the arrogant father-in-law of his beloved daughter. Jack Warner is a Six, and as such he's tremendously loyal not only to his family, but also to the police department. The prospect of helping his daughter's peace of mind, *and* helping society by jailing a criminal, gives Jack a great sense of anticipation.

And of course, a sense of uneasiness as well. There's a lot at stake here. But it's not like he's afraid or anything. He's not some cowardly weakling! No, he's going to storm right over to the suspect's house and start demanding some answers.

Oh, sure, Captain Ryan will probably warn him about being over-zealous, the way he always does when Jack gets impatient. Well, he can handle that. Captain might even be right, because Ryan's never yet called a case badly. But there's always the possibility of such a failure, and if that ever happens Jack knows what to do. Round up his fellow cops – at least the ones whose loyalty he's sure of – and get Ryan replaced.

First things first, though. Confront the suspect. It's the least he can do for Karen, who deserves all the security a loving father can provide. If she's worried about her father-in-law, Jack will come to the rescue. He's done that for twenty-six years now, and just because his daughter is married doesn't make her any less deserving of his protection.

So he heads over to the suspect's house, ready for whatever might happen next. Maybe the guy will deny everything and call in a lawyer. Maybe he'll pull a gun. Maybe he'll have the house wired to explode as soon as somebody knocks on the door, but that doesn't scare Jack. *Nothing* scares Jack, dammit! He's thought of every possible scenario, and he's ready for action.

Turns out the suspect calls a lawyer, which is kind of a letdown. Too much adrenaline to just sit here waiting for paperwork. But, say, speaking of paperwork – there may be an angle the blackmailer hasn't thought of. Jack knows every loophole in the system, so will this do the trick?

Maybe it will. Maybe it won't. Maybe this detective will break the case wide open through dogged preparation, or maybe he'll hesitate to take action for fear of being wrong.

Maybe he'll keep bouncing back and forth between worry and aggression, between listening to fear and drowning it out with action. Or maybe he'll reconcile both sides of his personality at just the right moment to save the day.

Your story. Your character. Your call.

= = = = = = = =

Next comes the princess trying to choose the best ally to defend her kingdom from an invasion of trolls – either the renegade dragon-rider, or the vampire lord.

As a Six, Aliana has already thought of every risk facing the kingdom. Maybe she's thought a little too long, because the trolls are only a day's march from the border, but she's been afraid of taking action prematurely.

What if that turns out to be the wrong move? Might there be some better option she just hasn't considered?

Her maid doesn't think so. Her maid is pushing for action, not seeming to realize that Aliana is facing the most enormous decision of her life. If only there were some way to *know* whether Kelwyn or Varek would be the safer choice.

Maybe she should talk to them both. After all, she's always been pretty good at winning people's loyalty. And while she's not sure whether loyalty matters to dragon-riders, she knows the vampire lord believes so strongly in loyalty that any betrayal would be unthinkable.

So, all right. Maybe she can make herself the kind of princess Varek will fall in love with. How hard could it be? Turn on the charm, blush when he pays her a compliment, laugh at anything that might seem the least bit fearsome so he'll never see any sign of weakness – she can do that. She's had plenty of practice.

Of course, there's that pesky business about the blood…and the very thought of it makes her skin cold. No, stop, think about something else. Think about how to save the kingdom. There are hundreds of peasants who've pledged to defend the castle with their very lives, and here she's getting squeamish over a little blood?

Maybe she'll approach the vampire lord, and hide any sign of fear so well that he'll believe he's getting an ally as strong as himself.

Or maybe he'll see right through her facade, which could lead to all kinds of other problems.

Maybe instead she'll strike up an alliance with the dragon-rider. Maybe things will go so beautifully that she's caught off guard. This is bad, this is dangerous – there has to be trouble just around the corner.

Maybe she'll realize that without a constant sense of tension, she's losing her sense of self. Maybe with the trolls' threat eliminated, she'll adopt a puppy for something to worry about. Maybe another attack will save her the trouble.

All we know for sure is that when things are at their worst, she'll rally and do whatever it takes to save the kingdom…because these are the people she loves.

= = = = = = = =

Now, here's our cowboy facing off against the cattle rustlers. Buck is a Six, so he's always prepared for trouble. He knows the first thing to do is to alert the sheriff, who's always taken a tough stand against outlaws.

In fact, Buck has been part of the volunteer posse ever since he came to the Triple C. He believes in their mission of keeping this part of the West safe for ranchers and families, and he's proud to do his part. The green bandana that marks him as a five-year volunteer is one of his greatest treasures.

So what if belonging to the posse means giving up his free time to patrol the town from midnight to four every morning? And who cares if ammunition has gotten so expensive that he can't afford to have his boots re-soled?

Those are minor sacrifices, and Buck is willing to pay any price for the good of his community.

But now he's beginning to wonder about the sheriff. Here the Triple C is being attacked by rustlers – the ranch hands have *seen* these bandits making off with their own branded cattle – and the sheriff is hemming and hawing. Saying maybe things will settle down with no intervention necessary. What kind of an attitude is that?

Well, Buck is a loyal member of the posse. Maybe the sheriff knows something he doesn't. Yeah, that's gotta be it. No point getting all worked up about this; no point wondering if he might've been wrong in trusting the man with the badge. After all, the sheriff knows more about catching rustlers than some ordinary cowboy. Makes sense, don't it?

A few more cattle vanish, and now Buck isn't so sure. Could it be that the sheriff he's always respected isn't really up to the job?

Seems wrong to even *think* that way, but here's all this evidence staring him in the face. And the idea that he's followed this man, he's taken pride in being part of the team which protects the community, when all the time the sheriff wasn't as trustworthy as everyone thought…well, that just burns. That ain't right!

By golly, he won't put up with this a minute longer. Buck's gonna round up everyone in the posse who thinks the same way *he* does about stamping out cattle rustlers, and lead them into action. Forget the sheriff, forget the midnight-to-four patrol. He's got a job to do, a ranch to protect, and on the way to catch those bandits – he's gonna wrap that stupid green bandana around a rock and hurl it through the sheriff's window. That'll make things clear.

Won't it?

= = = = = = = =

Let's take a look at the teenager whose only friend finds a buried treasure in the family's backyard.

It's a little unusual that Jamie has only one friend, because a Six will normally have a core of trusted companions. But let's say the family just moved here last month, school hasn't started yet, and Kelly is the only other teenager within a few miles of home.

So now there's this treasure, and Jamie isn't sure what to do. The money would come in handy, no question, because no matter how optimistic Mom tries to be they're still only one paycheck away from disaster. And Kelly is all in favor of selling their discovery on eBay, but that seems like a risky proposition.

Suppose it was buried by criminals who plan to return this week, and who'd wreak revenge on the entire household if the treasure is gone.

This isn't the kind of thing Mom can deal with, either. She's got enough to worry about with the move and the new job, and it's not like she always has the best advice in the world anyway. No, if anybody's going to protect the family from the returning criminals, it'll have to be Jamie.

Kelly reluctantly agrees to wait a week and see if anyone shows up at midnight to retrieve the chest. Jamie's relieved that it'll stay buried, because letting Kelly keep the treasure might not be so smart...they haven't been friends long enough to know for sure.

Sure, everything's just fine on the surface, and Kelly's already talking about driving to school together this fall, but it's hard to know who you can trust when everything looks fine. Better to wait and see.

Meanwhile, though, Jamie's getting more uneasy. Maybe the criminals returning is a little unlikely, but there are plenty of other possibilities to worry about.

Suppose the treasure was part of a trap set by government agents, and now they've spoiled the plan. Or what if a museum thought a year of aging would improve those emeralds, only to forget the location?

What if the rightful owners don't just knock on the door and explain the situation? What if they take some other, more drastic measures? What's Jamie supposed to *do*?

It'd help if there were someone in charge of a federal buried treasure department, but Jamie knows that isn't too likely. Maybe Kelly could ask around – somebody who's lived here longer might not arouse suspicion like a newcomer would – but it's hard to say for sure whether Kelly can be trusted. And somebody's gotta look out for Mom.... What's Jamie supposed to *do*?

= = = = = = = =

Finally, the career woman who hires a detective to find the baby she gave up for adoption 13 years ago. As a Six, Anne might have had any number of reasons for the adoption – let's say she didn't feel confident in her own child-rearing abilities, when there are so many things that could go wrong for even the best prepared parents.

But now she's discovered some rare disease which the adoptive parents must be warned about, and she knows that relying on the adoption caseworker isn't necessarily the safest move. If she wants to be absolutely certain her birth daughter is protected, she'll have to hire a private detective to find the child and deliver the news herself. Things can always go wrong, but doing this in person should offer the best guarantee of safety.

However, she hadn't counted on the growing attraction she feels for this detective. Craig is the kind of man she used to fantasize about, before realizing that building a career made more sense than pinning her hopes on some Prince Charming who might or might not materialize. Of course it'd be foolish to start hoping for any kind of a romance, but there's just something about him....

When she realizes he's attracted to her, as well, Anne is shaken. This is too good to be true, and she's only asking to be hurt if she opens her heart to this man. Why put herself through that kind of turmoil?

But Craig isn't put off when she insists their relationship is strictly business. He'll keep up the search for her daughter, but he's not going to let her pretend there's nothing between them. If she wants to stay just friends, that's fine, but he thinks they could be a lot more than friends.

Anne thinks so, too, and that scares her. She has a perfectly good life, she has a job she's good at and co-workers she enjoys and plenty of friends she's come to trust and value as if they were family. Why shake up her entire world just because a detective she's only known for three weeks makes her feel more...well, more alive?

Maybe Craig understands her reluctance to risk anything more than friendship. Maybe he takes offense and says if she can't imagine trusting him, she should hire some other detective. Maybe she continues struggling with doubt while they keep searching for her daughter, only to find Emily...who resents her birth mother, which breaks Anne's heart. Or maybe Emily is happy and healthy, showing Anne that tough decisions can work out beautifully, and that she *can* dare to love Craig. Whatever she decides is your pick!

Keep in mind that even if she changes her mind about trusting Craig, she's still a Six. A happier, healthier Six who's overcome the fatal flaw of fear – not trusting her own or anyone else's ability to handle whatever situation comes up – but a Six nonetheless.

Nobody changes their type. They can change their outlook on life, they can change the traits which have kept them from being the best they can be, but their fundamental type never changes.

Because remember how all nine types can be terrific people? A happy ending just means that this particular type has found their best self. A tragic ending means they've found it and turned away. An either-way ending means they haven't found it yet…but maybe they will in the next story.

You're the writer. You can pick. And readers who share your view of the world will be delighted with whatever choice you make.

CHAPTER SEVEN

QUIZ

- ☐ Do you like change?
- ☐ Are you generally at ease in groups?
- ☐ Do you try to avoid boredom at all costs?
- ☐ Do you dream about living The Good Life?
- ☐ Are you upbeat and enthusiastic?
- ☐ Do you like to make lots of plans?
- ☐ Are you frequently frustrated by rules and limitations?
- ☐ Do you seek out new and exciting experiences?
- ☐ Are you sometimes overly self-indulgent?
- ☐ Do you believe that if something is good, more is better?

___ **TOTAL FOR SEVEN**

TYPE SEVEN: The Adventurer, The Enthusiast, The Epicure

Think of Peter Pan, romping merrily through Neverland. Think of Rhett Butler, swashbuckling his way through the Civil War. Think of Auntie Mame, partying all through the Depression.

Could there be any better picture of a Seven?

Sevens look to the bright side. They enjoy new experiences, new adventures, new stimulation. If every moment of life could be a peak experience, Sevens would be supremely satisfied.

What they don't like is limits. Rules that constrict them from following their passion of the moment. Expectations that tie them down. Sevens love to be free, to wander wherever their fancy takes them, to do whatever strikes them as interesting on the spur of the moment.

They're connoisseurs of life. Given the choice of a three-course gourmet dinner or a full buffet, you know which they'd rather eat. They won't necessarily sample every single dish on the buffet line, but they love having the option to try whatever they want.

Nothing bothers Sevens more than seeing options disappear. Having to pick just one of anything frustrates them. Having to settle down in one place, do the same thing over and over, worry about the fine print, bores them. They'll do anything to avoid boredom, and if that means overindulging in the most convenient pleasures life has to offer, they won't hesitate to plunge in.

As long as they can stay in motion, they don't need to deal with anxiety. As long as they can find instant gratification just around the next corner, they'll happily celebrate every moment of every day. They prefer experiencing the environment, drinking in the marvels of new people and new sensations, rather than falling into a rut.

If you're having dinner with a group of Sevens for the first time, you'll feel like the most fascinating person in the world. They'll be hanging on your every word, drinking in everything you have to say, marveling at your outlook on life. Anything that's new will hold their attention, because there's such wonderful opportunity for excitement ahead.

If you spend the entire dinner reading the phone book, they'll *still* find you fascinating. "There must be something in the phone book we never spotted before!" "How do you decide where to start reading?" "Have you ever seen the same names twice in a row?"

Sevens can be wonderfully optimistic. They expect the best, and they frequently find it because of their genuine enthusiasm for whatever surrounds them. They'll go home raving about their fascinating new dinner companion who finds untapped depths in the phone book…but the next night at dinner, they'll go into equal raptures over someone who spends the entire evening punching calculator keys.

But if someone tells them they *have* to spend the evening dining with the greatest movie stars, Nobel prize winners and historic figures of all time, they'll balk. There's nothing Sevens hate more than commitment.

What if a better invitation comes along at the last minute? How can you expect them to cut off all their options? They resist anything that smacks of limitation, because that way lies the risk of boredom and – even worse – anxiety.

Sevens don't want to analyze their feelings. They'd rather be out doing things, having experiences, sampling new sensations. Philosophy isn't their strong suit, unless they view it as part of a grand adventure.

They'd rather not spend the time it takes to master the study of any single topic, when instead they could dabble in twenty topics during the same amount of time. Quantity, to them, is the very essence of quality.

This might turn them into dilettantes, or it might turn them into people who truly appreciate everything life has to offer. They like to keep things open-ended, giving themselves room to try more of whatever comes along. They love making plans for new experiences, even if they never follow through on the plans. What matters is the opportunity, the dazzling possibility of so many things just waiting to be tried...before they move onto the next.

Famous Sevens

Because Sevens are easily the most uninhibited and talkative of all the types, it's no surprise that their number includes so many top comedians and performers.

Look at the greats like Jack Benny, Robin Williams, Lily Tomlin, Bob Hope, Carol Burnett and John Belushi. Whether performing on stage or on screen, Sevens know how to energize an audience.

The same is true of musicians who bring something extra to their performance. Just listen to Barbra Streisand, Liberace, Bette Midler or Luciano Pavarotti. Or subtract the music and just listen to Larry King or Steve Allen. Moving from talk shows into politics and business, you can see the Seven's exuberant personality at work in people like John F. Kennedy, singer-turned-mayor Sonny Bono, and Malcolm Forbes.

Actors, of course, have that same larger-than-life quality, no matter what their era. You see it in classic movies featuring Clark Gable, Marlene Dietrich, Mickey Rooney, Ginger Rogers, Cary Grant and Elizabeth Taylor. You see it in TV reruns featuring Dick Van Dyke, Goldie Hawn, Jackie Gleason and Michael J. Fox. You see it in blockbusters starring Eddie Murphy, Jack Nicholson, Tom Hanks, Michael Caine and Brad Pitt.

You also see it in the work of directors like Martin Scorsese, Mel Brooks, Stephen Spielberg and Ron Howard...the choreography of Bob Fosse...the playing skills of Babe Ruth and Magic Johnson...and the "grabber" writing of Ray Bradbury, Judith Krantz, Kurt Vonnegut and Dave Barry. Different genres, but each author has that Seven ability to enthrall an audience, making readers feel privileged to watch the excitement unfolding before their very eyes.

Seven's Heroic Strengths

It's hard to resist the appeal of a character who takes delight in the entire world, who appreciates the very essence of life. Well-developed Sevens are so open to experience, so excited by the sensations that most people never stop to notice, that they can make everyday existence seem like the most captivating experience on earth.

A heroic Seven is something of a renaissance man or woman, multi-talented because of a sincere interest in hundreds of different things.

Their passion for life leads them to drink deeply of every possible experience, and their zest for adventure keeps them young at heart.

Sure, they might dive too deeply once in a while, but what's life *for* if not to enjoy?

Sevens are skilled at viewing every situation – and presenting it to others – in its best possible light.

Faced with a termite-ridden fence, they'll notice the intriguing gradations of color in old wood.

Faced with a grape-juice stain on the carpet, they'll decide that what this room has been missing is some colorful rugs.

Faced with company-wide layoffs, they'll focus on the marvelous new possibilities open to everyone whose job has vanished.

They're absolutely sincere in their bright-eyed outlook, but it can be annoying to others. How do Sevens deal with that? Cheerfully, of course.

"Sure, maybe people are upset about losing their jobs right *now*, but once they think it over they'll realize it's the best thing that could've happened."

Dealing with pain and loss isn't what Sevens do. They focus, instead, on the fun stuff. Someone who comes home and announces that "there may not be any more paychecks for a while, so we should celebrate this new lifestyle with a picnic on the beach" is definitely a Seven.

Seven's Fatal Flaws

Someone who wants to take in every possible experience can easily be accused of gluttony, and that's the fatal flaw of Sevens. As far as they're concerned, more is always better. If one perfect rose is beautiful, three dozen will be even more beautiful. If staying out until three in the morning is fun, all the more reason to stay out until four.

Sevens can fall into the habit of acquiring enjoyable new pursuits at such a rapid rate that they become consumers rather than connoisseurs. "That was fun; what's next?"

If they get to the point where nothing but excess seems like enough, they may find it hard to stop and simply smell the roses – even though they started out appreciating the glorious scent far more acutely than other types ever would.

Wanting to stay stimulated can make it tough for Sevens to concentrate on any particular thing long enough to get the most out of it. Staying on the move can be a way of constantly enjoying new experiences, but it can also be a way of avoiding depth...because depth might involve some pain, and Sevens just don't want to deal with pain.

In fact, they frequently wind up moving whenever things get rough. Better a new job than to deal with a boring boss. Better a new friend than to face a request for commitment. Better a new town than one where they've already sampled every restaurant.

So, obviously, the biggest roadblock for Sevens isn't gluttony, but rather their use of gluttony to avoid making tough decisions.

A character who recognizes that it's pretty much impossible to keep every option open, and who decides instead to stay put and deal with the situation at hand, is one who's well on the way to a happy ending.

Sevens As Children

Children tend to be more focused on their own world than that of others, and this is especially true of Sevens. They're free spirits, so good-natured that their friends will overlook any little flaws like not showing up for a promised play date.

Like their adult counterparts, little Sevens prefer to avoid dealing with pain or need. But as long as no one is demanding long-term devotion, they're delightful companions. They enjoy activities more if there's company on board, but if their friends want to take some path besides their choice for the day, they'll cheerfully go their own way.

Parents who expect a conventional, obedient child may have a hard time dealing with energetic, resourceful Sevens. These children are likely to demand more freedom than most, and possibly more freedom than they can handle.

The wise parents are those who encourage a frustrated Seven to find some new interest, some new area of exploration which can provide a whole fresh sense of adventure.

Charm is part of the Seven's makeup, and it enables these children to make their way through the world with goodwill all around. Since they're good with language, excellent talkers, they can frequently ease their way out of an uncomfortable situation by telling a joke. Or a lie, if that works better.

These children are skilled at finessing their way around adults, and at re-framing any situation for the most enjoyable outcome. Enneagram theorist Helen Palmer describes a Seven who gets caught raiding the cookie jar, and who immediately accuses the jar owner of having a small-minded attitude toward snacking. The discussion moves from the unimportance of a few crumbs to the importance of global nutrition, at which point the Seven strolls away…laden with cookies!

Sevens At Work

The most popular person in the workplace is likely to be a Seven. That's because they're easy to get along with, and they make a point of seeing the best in everyone. If somebody does a bad job, Seven is quicker to forgive than most types…because why dwell on the negative?

They're also very good at coming up with ideas. But when it comes to following through, they lose interest. Brainstorming, not implementation, is Seven's strength.

The worst job imaginable for a Seven would be doing exactly the same thing, hour after hour. They'd far rather sell a product than construct it, and they're great at presenting any product in its best possible light.

If a company could choose only one person to be its public face, the best choice is almost always a Seven – because Sevens are genuinely interested in building goodwill among everyone they meet.

They'd far rather work in some environment where everyone is equal. While they might dress it up with talk of egalitarianism, the fact is that they don't want anyone bossing them around.

If there are rules about filling out a request form to get pencils, the Seven is likely to take more of a big-picture viewpoint and explain that since the goal is to avoid wasting pencils, and filling out the request form requires using pencil lead, it'll save money to just skip the form.

Such creative thinking is typical of Sevens, and shows why they perform well in an emergency. They're good at thinking on their feet, and won't hesitate to take action. They're also good at maintaining a sense of enthusiasm which energizes those around them.

Just don't expect them to fill out the pencil request form.

Sevens In Relationships

Anyone who resists commitment might seem like an unlikely prospect for a satisfying long-term relationship. But in fact, Sevens can be wonderful lifelong friends, partners and even spouses – as long as they don't feel tied down.

With so many interests and passions and experiences already collected, it's pretty easy for the Seven to find common ground with virtually everyone.

They automatically assume that each new person they meet will be wonderfully fascinating, and they'll enjoy that person fully…at least for the moment. If the relationship continues, it's because the Seven continues to find this person fascinating.

What drives them away is boredom, a sense of limitation, or a demand for sharing some painful trauma. Sevens are willing to share all kinds of experiences, but not emotional pain. They'd rather stay focused on the good times. Someone who wants to maintain a lifelong relationship will improve the odds by giving the Seven a feeling of freedom – and also indicating that emotional depth isn't such a terrible thing.

Because Sevens like to keep things breezy, they'll resist any sort of confrontation.

If they're challenged to defend themselves, they'll take what they consider to be the high ground: "I'm open to the world; you're close-minded. You don't understand; you're not even trying to see things from a broader perspective." But when they feel understood, they're happy to share their lives with anyone whose interests match their own.

Once a Seven is willing to trade the excitement of unlimited options for the satisfaction of an ongoing relationship, they're great companions.

And even if they show up only once a year to suggest a movie featuring the obscure actor you both admire, that once-a-year event will be consistently enjoyable. That's what Sevens are all about.

Seven's Individual Subtype

When it comes to self-preservation, Sevens are most likely to find that in the company of people who think the same way they do.

They'll seek out friends who share their view of life, creating a virtual family – if not an actual one – of great, compatible companions.

If this Seven is surrounded by family members who share an optimistic outlook and preference for new experiences, spending more time at home is only logical. Everyone can enjoy planning vacations and reminiscing about them, as much as the actual vacation itself.

Planning becomes a bigger part of the individual Seven's life, because it matters that like-minded people are always within easy reach. So while most Sevens prefer to do things on the spur of the moment, one who's oriented toward self-preservation will phone ahead to make sure those essential friends and family members are ready for company.

It's easy for this Seven to take on the job of keeping everyone entertained, and natural to do that job brilliantly. It's also likely that since not every friend shares the exact same interests, the Seven will have a long list of friends who share certain passions – one who enjoys soccer games, one who enjoys shopping, one who enjoys Thai food – and seek them out periodically. If they haven't seen each other for two years, no problem. The Seven just assumes they're still friends. Why wouldn't they be?

Seven's Intimacy Subtype

Sevens love sharing excitement with someone who appreciates each new experience. So those with the intimacy subtype are likely to seek out partners who'll match their zest for life.

They'll start the relationship with tremendous enthusiasm, expecting to like and be liked with equal passion. They're sincerely interested in each new person, until the relationship begins to feel ordinary.

Then comes the risk of boredom…but the intimacy subtype knows how to avoid that. It's simply a matter of viewing the other person in a more romantic context than before.

Even so, that might not be quite as fulfilling as the first spark of attraction. And it's incredibly easy for a Seven to meet and charm new people. So why hang onto a relationship that's run its course? Seek out a new one instead.

It's hard for anyone who likes keeping every option open to settle for just one city, one job, one mate. Sevens who indulge in gluttony for intense one-on-one relationships will participate wholeheartedly as long as things stay exciting. But if someone starts expecting a commitment, they'd just as soon not hang around. After all, there are so many wonderful people out there.

And most of these people enjoy the Seven, too. How can they resist someone who's always fun, who forgives easily and who rarely passes judgment? Even if such a relationship doesn't endure, it's always a pleasure while it lasts.

Seven's Social Subtype

Putting the social group first is a natural choice for Sevens who enjoy the company of others – as long as those others like the same things they do.

It's not hard to find like-minded people when you're as versatile as the Seven, so the social-subtype Sevens rarely have trouble fitting into a group.

Of course, if belonging to the group involves any emotional turmoil, they won't stick around.

If belonging to the group requires following a certain set of rules, they'll move along quickly. If belonging to the group means taking responsibility for people around them, they'll say a cheerful goodbye and take off.

But if the group upholds Sevens' ideal of an egalitarian society, where everyone is equally valuable and nobody gets bossed around, they'll happily take part in every possible activity.

In fact, if their ideals are the same as those of their fellow members, they'll dive into participation with every ounce of energy they've got.

Sevens are willing to risk everything for a cause they believe in, and they don't see any need to sit around talking about it. Just jump in and get the job done.

If a group gets bogged down in procedural chit-chat, though, Sevens won't stay for long. They know what they want to do, and there's no point waiting for a consensus when they can do it with some other group instead.

Sevens With Other Types

Sevens are great at sharing their enthusiasm for adventure, but that doesn't provide much conflict for an author. Instead, take a look at what can go wrong when a Seven encounters any of the nine types.

Seven & One

Seven wants to let the details take care of themselves. One wants to make sure all the details are taken care of. "Look, if you'd just lighten up once in a while…" "Look, if you'd just take some responsibility once in a while…"

Seven & Two

Here's where the desire for freedom meets the desire to nurture. "You're obsessing about our relationship," says Seven. "I just want to know where you stand," says Two, "so can't you give me some clue?" "Can't you give me some *space*?"

Seven & Three

They're both big-picture thinkers. They both enjoy planning swell activities. But either one can get wrapped up in something which results in ignoring the other, and feel frustrated when the other doesn't *get* their excitement.

Seven & Four

Seven feels strangled and wants to get out when Four is in pain. Four wants emotional sustenance which Seven can't provide: "I can't keep looking on the dark side." "If you cry with me we'll both feel better." "It won't work."

Seven & Five

"Oh, boy," says Seven, "a party!" "No, thanks, you go." "Come on, it'll be fun!" "I'd rather stay home and read." "Don't you want to be with me?" "At a *party*?" "We never have any fun." "We have great privacy." "What about our *life*?"

Seven & Six

"It might rain," Six frets. "So, it'll be fun to get wet. You worry too much." "You don't worry enough." "I'm just trying to keep things fun." "Oh, you're saying I'm a party-pooper?" "Why do you always have to look at the dark side?"

Seven & Seven

"There's a new roller-coaster opening tomorrow – let's go ride it." "Sounds like fun, but I might be busy." "Yeah, I might be too, so forget it." "Thing is, it *would* be more fun with company." "Maybe I'll be there, maybe I won't."

Seven & Eight

Seven won't put up with Eight's anger, and Eight won't put up with Seven's attempt to avoid confrontations with charm. "We need to sit down and talk about this." "Maybe tomorrow." "No, right now." "So long, I'm outta here."

Seven & Nine

"So many options," says Seven. "I know," Nine agrees, "what should we pick?" "This might be good, but so might that." "Or that, or that…." "Well, let's quit pondering and *do* something." "You're always pushing me," says Nine.

You see how none of these is a life-and-death conflict? But each one can be intensified or relieved, depending on where you are in the story.

Some conflicts may strike you as overly dramatic or overly boring. That's okay. That's a clear sign that your story doesn't *need* such a conflict. You may have enough conflict already. If you do need more, though, it's a safe bet that at least one of these examples will spark some ideas. And that's where the fun begins.

Scenarios With Sevens

No matter what kind of story you're telling, the characters' personality types will make a difference in the conflict that arises.

Here are examples of five stories – about a detective, a princess, a cowboy, a teenager and a career woman – where the protagonist will come into conflict because of his or her enneagram type.

= = = = = = = =

Let's start with the cop trying to track down a blackmailer who's threatening the arrogant father-in-law of his beloved daughter. Jack Warner is a Seven, so we know he's great at coming up with creative ways to trap blackmailers. Or drug dealers. Or murderers, arsonists and petty thieves.

The more options, the better. Jack will volunteer for any new assignment that comes along, since a fresh perspective is better than the same-old-routine viewpoint of cops who work only one type of case.

And he's handled some fascinating cases over the years. What, eleven years already? Nobody ever thought he'd stay on the job *that* long, and he's even surprised himself. But that's the great thing about police work – there's always something new.

And right now the new assignment is to catch this blackmailer. Jack can't figure out why Karen's father-in-law waited to seek help, unless maybe he was just hoping the whole thing would go away by itself. Which makes sense. No point courting trouble when most things do get better by themselves. Or at least some things.

Like his relationship with Karen. His daughter used to complain when he missed a school play or birthday party, and Jack had a hard time convincing her that sometimes things come up at the last minute. But lately she's gotten more relaxed about family dinners and such. When he had to leave early last Thanksgiving, she just fixed him a plate to go. Great daughter. Jack's crazy about her.

So the least he can do for her is help bail out her father-in-law, even though the guy can be a pain sometimes. Always acting like there's only one way to do things, when Jack knows that's not true. Anyway, might as well get to work and see what he can come up with.

There are a few distractions, which make the day more interesting, but within half an hour Jack comes up with a plan. The details, he can hand over to Kane or Taylor...they're both good at figuring out fine points. Jack's better at the big picture, and it disturbs him when Taylor explains that the only way for this plan to succeed is for Jack to monitor the suspect's recorded conversations.

This is boring. This isn't the kind of work he was cut out for. Okay, maybe he's the only cop who's ever heard the victim's voice, but does that mean he's gotta sit here listening to recordings for hours on end? A guy could go nuts, spending a whole day like this.

And yet he promised Karen he'd work the case.... What's he gonna do?

Well, he's your cop. So he'll do whatever gives you the best story!

= = = = = = = =

Next comes the princess trying to choose the best ally to defend her kingdom from an invasion of trolls – either the renegade dragon-rider, or the vampire lord.

Aliana's pretty good at getting people to see things her way, so she's not too worried about winning the allegiance of either Kelwyn or Varek. The only hard part is deciding which one to pick. Here she's got two great possibilities before her, but no matter which one she chooses she'll have lost the other forever.

Well, maybe she can postpone the decision. Of course she doesn't want to see the trolls start killing peasants, because so many of those peasants are wonderful people, but there can't be any harm in waiting a little while. Things could change. You never know.

Besides, how did it come to be *her* job to protect the kingdom, anyway? She never asked for this responsibility. She would've been perfectly happy taming her unicorn, designing tapestries with her handmaidens, and coming up with new ways to disguise herself for the jousting tournaments. But no, along comes this invasion, and now she's stuck.

Unless maybe she can find someone else to take over the job. Couldn't the steward handle it? Well, no, he's drunk most of the time. Or maybe the wizard, except she hasn't seen him in a while. Aliana envies his ability to disappear whenever things get sticky, and wishes she had some of that skill herself. But no, she's the princess and the trolls are on the march and she's got to make some kind of decision.

Suppose she lets the dragon-rider and the vampire lord work things out by themselves. Invite them both to dinner, explain the situation, and mention that it'd be very handy to have an ally. Yes, they've sworn to kill one another if they ever meet face to face, but she's good at keeping people happy. Get some harpists in, some wine, turn the entire castle into the kind of place people can't help but enjoy.

Oh, except the vampire lord won't settle for wine. Hmm, that might be a problem.

All right, then, maybe she can convince the trolls to march someplace else. Why risk losing either of her potential allies if she doesn't have to? There's no point in limiting her options, is there?

Better yet, maybe she can announce that the kingdom is free territory. No ruler at all, so there'll be nothing for the trolls to overthrow. Everyone can do as they please, which the peasants should certainly enjoy. She can get back to her unicorn. Or maybe her tapestry. Or maybe that new garden....

= = = = = = = =

Now, here's our cowboy facing off against the cattle rustlers. Buck is a Seven, so he's probably the most popular cowboy in the bunkhouse. If it's just a matter of rounding up enough fellows to keep watch all night, there won't be any problem convincing 'em to stay awake.

Except that doesn't seem to be doing the trick, and now Buck is getting annoyed. No problem missing a night's sleep here and there – he's done that often enough – but in the past it's always been for a good cause. Well, stopping rustlers is a good cause, too, but it's sure not what anyone would call fun.

Okay, look at it another way. This is a contest, right? Him versus the rustlers, and it'll be a really challenging game. Games are always interesting, and Buck's enjoyed quite a few evenings of poker at the saloon. So this is more of the same, right?

No, drat it, playing poker is more entertaining because there are people all around. Keeping watch alone isn't quite the same thing.

Maybe instead, it'll be like one of those stories his pa used to tell. Somebody named Leatherstocking, sneaking around in the woods. Buck wouldn't mind an adventure like that, especially if it means coming face to face with a rustler.

Except the rustlers don't seem to be showing up. He should've brought along some grub, or a chaw of tobacco, or even a bottle of sarsaparilla – Miss Lillian is partial to sarsaparilla, and maybe he could ride into town long enough to convince her to keep him company.

She might not want to stay out late, because as the schoolmarm she's always worried about her reputation, but there are plenty of other gals at the saloon. Buck shouldn't have any problem finding one who'd enjoy some entertainment tonight.

Of course, Miss Lillian wouldn't be too happy about that. Somehow she's gotten the idea that she and Buck have an understanding, which he isn't too sure about.

It's not like he ever asked her to marry him, not in so many words. Sure, she's fun to be with, and he likes her better than any of those saloon gals, but spending the rest of his life with just one woman seems like a crazy idea.

Might be kind of interesting for a change, but there's no rush. Life's fine the way it is.

If only those dratted rustlers would show up. Why didn't he bring some of that cornbread, anyway? The Triple C cook makes better cornbread than anybody in three counties, and –

Wait, is that a sound? Yeah, by golly, the rustlers are coming. Finally, some action! Buck's ready, all right. More than ready. Let 'em come.

= = = = = = = =

Let's take a look at the teenager whose only friend finds a buried treasure in the family's backyard.

Jamie would normally have far more than one friend. For a Seven, making friends is the easiest thing in the world – there are so many people with interesting stories, and everyone seems to like Jamie. But the family only moved in two days ago, everyone's been cooped up with chores, and it was a relief when Kelly from next door showed up yesterday. Life is always better when you've got a friend around.

At least Jamie hopes so. Things got off to a great start, because the minute Kelly started helping with the garden there was that thunk of metal which began the greatest adventure of the month. Maybe even the year.

But then Kelly started talking about responsibility, about searching for the rightful owner before they can claim the treasure for themselves. Jamie can't see the point. If somebody really wanted those jewels, they would've kept 'em safe in the first place. Besides, the whole idea of buried treasure is to enrich the people who found it.

If people care about keeping their money, they use it to buy stocks or something. Whoever buried those jewels was more interested in excitement, and Jamie's all in favor of that.

Kelly just doesn't understand the appeal of a possible mystery, a possible triumph, a possible adventure. Which means Jamie hasn't explained it clearly enough, because why else would someone refuse the chance for a million dollars? Or maybe two million. Or three. Even if it's only half a million, the principle is the same. Here's a fortune they can use for whatever they want. What's not to love about that?

Jamie's already got dozens of plans for half the fortune, and will be glad to help Kelly plan for the other half as well. They could start by taking a trip to New York. Mom and Dad might worry, but once they see that Jamie's got the money to pay for a limo and a hotel suite, they're bound to understand. Maybe even come along...limos can hold a dozen people, right? Bring the whole family, why not? If they pass any hitchhikers who might be down on their luck, invite them along. The more, the merrier!

So the only problem is convincing Kelly that there's no need to advertise this treasure in the Lost & Found section. If it belonged to someone poor and hungry, that'd be different, but poor and hungry people wouldn't have jewels like that in the first place. Jamie just needs to explain things better, and then the fun can begin....

= = = = = = = =

Finally, the career woman who hires a detective to find the baby she gave up for adoption 13 years ago. As a Seven, Anne might have had any number of reasons for the adoption – let's say she knew Emily would be better off with full-time parents than a single mom who'd never held down a job for more than a month or two.

But now she's discovered some rare disease which the adoptive parents must be warned about, and she knows it wouldn't be fair to keep the news to herself. The best thing she can do is hire a detective to find Emily. No reason for her to get involved personally, because it might be distressing for all concerned. What if the girl never knew she was adopted? What if the parents wanted to keep it a secret? Better to let the detective handle everything, and concentrate on her other projects instead.

For some reason, though, Craig's first report intrigues her. He announces that the adoptive parents were tremendously grateful for the news; they've always told Emily how much her birth mom must've loved her, and now they'd all like to meet Anne in person.

Well, this might be interesting. Nobody's expecting anything in particular, so why not take some time off and go meet the family?

Craig offers to accompany her, which pleases Anne. He's appealed to her sense of adventure ever since they met...and now, there's no longer any detective-client relationship in the way. They might as well enjoy themselves.

But after only a few days together, she's starting to feel uneasy. This man is more intriguing than anyone she's ever met, and somehow she suspects it'll be harder to say goodbye than it's ever been before. Even worse, he seems to think they might have some kind of a future together. As tempting as that might sound right now, Anne knows it would be a mistake. She can't ever settle down with one person, give up all the spontaneous freedom she's spent a lifetime pursuing, and why can't Craig understand that?

Then they meet Emily, and she's astonished at how much the girl resembles herself at that age. Maybe Emily's passion for independence confirms that she's right to feel the same way. Or maybe it strikes her as appropriate for a child, but no longer the most satisfying choice for a grown woman. Maybe Craig takes them both fishing and shows his own carefree side, which reassures Anne that they *could* share an exciting life together. Or maybe she says goodbye and finds herself missing him so much that she flees to a new city for a new life.

Keep in mind that even if she decides to settle down with Craig, she's still a Seven. A happier, healthier Seven who's overcome the fatal flaw of gluttony – wanting nothing but new experiences every moment of each day – but a Seven nonetheless.

Nobody changes their type. They can change their outlook on life, they can change the traits which have kept them from being the best they can be, but their fundamental type never changes.

Because remember how all nine types can be terrific people? A happy ending just means that this particular type has found their best self. A tragic ending means they've found it and turned away. An either-way ending means they haven't found it yet…but maybe they will in the next story.

You're the writer. You can pick. And readers who share your view of the world will be delighted with whatever choice you make.

CHAPTER EIGHT

QUIZ

- ☐ Do you feel you can handle conflict easily?
- ☐ Do you respect assertive people?
- ☐ Are you more a leader than a follower?
- ☐ Do people describe you as earthy, blunt and straightforward?
- ☐ Is pretense disturbing to you?
- ☐ Is it easy for you to get in touch with your anger?
- ☐ Do you believe in fighting for what is right?
- ☐ Would you rather be respected than liked?
- ☐ Do people think of you as courageous?
- ☐ Do you find it easy to assert yourself?

___ **TOTAL FOR EIGHT**

TYPE EIGHT: The Leader, The Controller, The Boss

Protecting the weak. Standing up for truth and justice. The courage to challenge powerful forces and make things better for everyone. We're talking an inspired crusader, right?

Right. We're also talking an Eight.

Eights are the people who guard their soft, vulnerable center behind a wall of power and strength. They're natural leaders who won't hesitate to offer guidance when people need direction – and sometimes even when people don't.

Their self-confidence comes from knowing their own strength, like a warrior who could wipe out every enemy with a flick of the sword and thus can afford to be gentle and calm.

So when you find someone who's not afraid to step up as a leader, who's not afraid to deliver an honest opinion, who's not afraid of what people might think, you've likely found an Eight.

Eights don't see much point in sitting around pondering, or getting all emotional, when they could just as well take action. But behind their "let's get down to playing and *win*" mentality, Eights still retain a childlike innocence. They're highly receptive to the beauties of nature, and they can draw tremendous spiritual strength from spending time by the sea or in the garden or desert or woods.

In fact, they're so aware of their own fragility – as compared to the majesty of the earth – that they vow to protect and guard whatever needs defending, whether it's a forest or a friend. They have no problem standing up to a bully or a boss or a braggart who's picking on someone weaker, because they view it as their job to make sure that nobody uses power unfairly.

Although they can slip up in that area. Say a group of Eights decide it's their job to wipe out evil, money-grubbing landlords so all children will have a safe place to sleep.

They might do it by filing a lawsuit against exorbitant rents and inspiring everyone in town to raise money for a children's shelter. Or they might do it by smashing the roof of the landlord's car and threatening worse unless he straightens things out.

Either way, though, Eights will approach the problem with sheer, direct honesty. They never dissemble. They put themselves right out there, explaining who they are and what they want and what they're going to do.

An Eight can't imagine whispering malicious gossip about someone who wore the wrong shoes or failed to repay a loan. Why not just announce, "Hey, your shoes don't match" or ask, "When are you going to pay me back?"

Such straightforwardness appeals to people who appreciate knowing that what they see is what they get. It may also alienate people who prefer doing things more subtly. But Eights see no point in changing to try and influence anyone. They are who they are, and that's that.

The only thing they might hide from is their own vulnerable side. Remember the movie scene where the little girl shares her flowers with the Frankenstein monster? He's looking amazed, then worried that this brief interlude of happiness can't last long, and finally simply enjoying the beauty of the moment.

That's a perfect sketch of an Eight.

But because Eights don't always acknowledge the core of softness within themselves, they sometimes become fixated on power. The best defense is a good offense, so they'll make a point of challenging rules and being first in line and refusing to consider that they might be wrong. These less-evolved Eights are more afraid of weakness and being controlled than those who've realized they *can* let down their guard here and there.

An Eight who's willing to allow some sensitivity becomes far stronger, because now there's nothing to be afraid of. They're still full of energy, great at figuring out what needs to get done and plowing into it at top speed, but they're willing to trust other people and listen to new ideas. They've earned their self-confidence, and you can see it radiating from them whenever they walk into a room.

Famous Eights

Eights are good at saying what they think, not beating around the bush or waiting for someone else to state an opinion so they'll know which way the wind blows. You see that in political figures like Golda Meir, Lyndon Johnson and Indira Gandhi, as well as in commentators like Mike Wallace, Rush Limbaugh and Barbara Walters.

They're also great at sports, because their fierce energy isn't held back by worries about whether they'll win or lose. They play to win, but their self-esteem is strong enough that a loss doesn't haunt them.

Legends like Ty Cobb, Evel Knievel and Billie Jean King embody that kind of drive. So do Charles Barkley, John McEnroe, George Foreman and Jimmy Connors.

Eights are willing to fight for what they believe in, whether the battle is verbal or physical or both. Look at Generals George Patton and Charles de Gaulle, heroes of World War II. Malcolm X, Eldridge Cleaver and Martin Luther King, who each stood up for change in whatever way seemed most effective under the circumstances.

Entertainers with an Eight personality never hide behind a press agent or a public relations script. Whether they're as subtle as Michael Douglas and Sean Connery or as blatant as Lee Marvin, Bea Arthur and John Wayne, they don't hesitate to put themselves wholeheartedly into their roles.

Ernest Hemingway showed that same cards-on-the-table style. Same with Frank Sinatra. Same with Donald Trump. Eights are always willing to take a risk, to speak without hedging their bets, and to let the chips fall where they may.

Eight's Heroic Strengths

No other type has the self-confidence of an Eight. These people know they can make their way in the world, and that gives them the moral and physical courage to look out for those who can't.

The image of a knight is highly appropriate. For Eights, the armor might not be metal-plated…it may come more from knowing they can handle whatever life throws their way.

Once they decide you're on their team, they'll defend you to the death. Literally. My husband is an Eight, and he can't understand why I'd hesitate to throw myself in front of a speeding truck if that'd save a child in the way. Who cares if the kid's a stranger? Somebody's gotta take action!

If Eights are willing to go to bat for strangers, they're even more supportive of their loved ones. They're good at building your self-esteem, because their own convictions are so strong. "Of *course* you're a great person. Believe me. It's the truth."

Truth matters to an Eight. If the truth is uncomfortable, so be it…they can stand discomfort. What they can't stand is pretense, affectation or phony cordiality.

Still, strong Eights are capable of tremendous self-restraint, and only the most acute observer might notice the smoldering volcano beneath the calm surface. Eights who are confident in their own power can be charismatic leaders, refusing to throw their weight around – unless that's what it takes to protect someone else.

Eights enjoy taking on a challenge, because it keeps them connected to the intensity of life. It's hard to find an Eight who'd rather spend the weekend watching TV indoors if there's a chance for excitement just down the street. Don the armor, grab the flag… there's a quest waiting!

Eight's Fatal Flaws

Lust is the Eight's fatal flaw. Lust for power, lust for excitement, lust for activity and challenge and purpose – more of it, right here, right now.

Eights like to live large. They don't mind seeking out the wild side of life, and if that means taking big risks or attempting perilous feats or sampling unknown substances, no problem...they can handle it. They're used to handling whatever comes up, so what's one more danger? Bring it on.

The Eights who haven't made peace with their inner vulnerability will lose no time proving that life can't offer any obstacles greater than a powerful will. They want to be the biggest and best, the one everybody looks up to, and they see no point in sharing power. They'd rather just declare how they want things done, and if that means intimidating a few annoying folks who don't want to go along, bring 'em on.

Of course this makes it hard to trust anyone, because you never know who might disagree. Eights don't have to worry about another Eight trying any sneaky, back-stabbing maneuvers, because they're not the type who'd resort to such treachery. But other types...better to watch your back.

Softness is okay in babies and kittens, but not in the Eights who lust for control. They can't let down their guard, and they're always aware of everyone else's strengths and weaknesses. If it looks like you're going to attack, they'd better attack first. Get there ahead of the others. Do whatever it takes to defend their position.

So you can see the dramatic potential of an Eight considering whether to give up the lust for power and trust another person. It can be a tremendously exciting turnaround – exciting enough, in fact, to thrill even a guarded Eight.

Eights As Children

Even as children, Eights may perceive themselves as being the strongest in the family. Sometimes they are. In a family where one of the children seems to manage the entire household, that child is likely an Eight.

This young Eight might be a loner, or might have dozens of friends. If so, those friends will never have to worry about being protected from bullies or gossips or unfair teachers. The Eight won't stand for it.

Same as the adult Eights, these children love to face challenges. They'll feel disappointed if there's never any opportunity for heroism, for saving the day, for triumphing over evil.

Whether it's ensuring that the new kid gets a place in the cafeteria line or standing up to a teacher whose assignment didn't make sense, Eights are always willing to stand up and speak out. Their strong, independent spirit won't allow for anything else.

Their natural exuberance may bewilder grandparents who expected a quiet, polite little visitor. If Grandma doesn't like noise, too bad. But if Mom or Dad explains that Grandma needs quiet because she's recovering from surgery, the young Eight will be careful to whisper and tiptoe around the house.

Of course, Mom and Dad had better be telling the truth. Eights expect honesty, and they reward it with integrity. They might flat-out refuse to attend a party hosted by some kid they don't like, but they'll never lie about their motivation.

They might need some practice learning when to express their anger and when to count to ten, but parents who encourage the ability to compromise – and who enforce *only* those rules for which there's a genuinely good reason – will be rewarded with a child who respects the value of cooperation.

Eights At Work

Eights love the chance to meet problems head-on. They're always willing to accept responsibility for a tough assignment, and they're good at taking the initiative.

Because these people tend to be self-motivated, they may find it hard to work for somebody else. Eights are happier when they control their own destiny, and the risks of running their own business don't bother them. In fact, if they're responsible for any project, they'll do a better job when the goals are clearly defined and everyone gets out of the way to let them work.

Eights don't mind working for someone they admire, but they'd much rather take charge than take orders from someone they don't respect. They'll gladly go head-to-head with a worthy opponent, and won't hesitate to offer a handshake at the end of a fair contest. They don't carry a grudge, and find it hard to understand why other people do. Hidden agendas aren't part of an Eight's personality.

However, they'll never follow the rules just because somebody decreed it. Life is too short to worry about rules that don't make sense.

They'll have no problem stopping for a red light at a busy intersection, but if it's three in the morning and no other cars are in sight? There's no point in burning gas, just sitting there. Eights value practical truths more than social correctness.

At their worst, they'll view compromise as a weakness and insist that their way is the only way. At their best, they'll hold out for clarity and full disclosure so that everyone gets a fair deal. Either way, they'll work as hard as they can for any cause they believe in and never stop in midstream to wonder whether they might be better off somewhere else.

Eights In Relationships

Eights bring the passion, the intensity and the excitement to any relationship they're in. Once they've decided you're trustworthy, you'll have a staunch ally for life.

But earning the trust of an Eight might take some time. They're so resistant to being controlled that they won't let down their guard until they *know* it's safe to relax around you and show their weaker side. Consistent honesty and dependability is the only way to earn their trust, but the reward is lifelong honesty and dependability in return.

Inside the Eight's guarded perimeter, you'll find generosity and possessiveness, loyalty and bluntness, integrity and arrogance all rolled into one. Eights will never be underhanded or sneaky, but neither will they hold back from making demands. If you refuse to meet a particular demand, they won't hold it against you. Instead they'll respect you for not giving in, and find some other way of getting what they want. After all, if you gave in it would mean you'd betrayed your own values, and that's the last thing they'd ask from a loved one.

Eights are used to relying on their own instincts and willpower and strength, so committing to a long-term relationship is a challenge for them.

Once they've done it, though, they're steadily supportive, generous and truthful. You're on their side. They care about you. They'll defend you against anything, and expect the same kind of loyalty in return. If physical or verbal defense isn't your strong suit, that's okay…they'll settle for what you *can* give.

They like to be appreciated for what they are, but not flattered with praise they haven't earned. And they give the same veracity in return. When an Eight admires something about you, you know it's the wholehearted truth.

Eight's Individual Subtype

The Eight who values self-preservation wants to have enough of everything. Maybe not a hoard of canned goods in the pantry, but it's important to know where to *get* canned goods in case of emergency. When some useful item they've come to depend on is unavailable, it throws them for a loop.

They hate the idea of not being able to take care of themselves. They don't want to have to rely on anyone else for basic necessities, or even for fun little extras.

They want the security of being completely independent, knowing they can protect themselves and their homes and the people they love.

One way of ensuring such protection is to always sit with their back to the wall. They feel better if they can see the entire environment around them, because there's less risk of a surprise attack. Maybe the attack is only from Aunt Mary demanding, "Why weren't you in church yesterday?" but even so, the Eight wants to preserve control over the situation.

Losing control is unnerving. And the best way to maintain control is to stay tough. Physically, mentally, emotionally, whatever it takes to survive. As long as there's plenty of emergency gear available, as long as the essential creature comforts – and maybe a few luxuries – are within easy reach, then self-preservation is assured.

Eight's Intimacy Subtype

The only way an Eight will surrender control to someone else in a relationship is to feel absolutely certain of the other person's intentions.

That might take a while. It might involve a few calculated risks, like sharing a potentially embarrassing secret and waiting to see if the secret gets leaked. But even when Eights feel safe and loved, it's hard to give up the habit of command.

> **Their ideal partner would be someone who lets them be in charge at all times, combined with someone who'll stand up to them whenever they step out of line.**

Of course they'll never find such a relationship, but that doesn't mean they can't enjoy the search. In fact, the chase may be far more satisfying than actually settling down together. Eights who value relationships appreciate the electric energy of high-voltage arguments more than the dull drone of everyday comfort.

If they're willing to share their own vulnerabilities, they expect the same in return. They love deeply, and if they feel betrayed they're very slow to forgive. They'll forgive a knock-down, drag-out fight ten seconds after it's over, because a fight is truthful. Nobody's hiding anything.

They appreciate honesty. They appreciate hearing what people think, as long as these are people they've decided to let into their guarded shell. Anyone who's managed to get close to an Eight will be assured of a lifelong relationship…as long as the trust endures.

Eight's Social Subtype

Eights who emphasize their relationship with a group, family or society are very much like those who emphasize their relationship with an individual. The first order of business is to determine whether they're safe in offering their trust. Because if ever it's betrayed, they're gone.

But once they understand the group's power structure and where everyone's loyalties lie, they'll cheerfully take on the role of a protector. They're loyal to everyone who's on board, wanting the best for everyone in the group and determined to look out for anyone who needs it – although they'll work with whoever seems weak in order to build up their self-confidence and strength.

If the group is based on some righteous struggle, the social-subtype Eights will joyfully embrace a common purpose and throw themselves into working for justice.

They'll reserve any hostility or anger for outside forces that might threaten the welfare of the group. Belonging means keeping everyone safe to the best of their ability, and knowing everyone else will do the same.

Whether the society they support is their own family or a group of friends, Eights take their responsibility very seriously. They enjoy the camaraderie of people who want the best for one another, and hold themselves accountable for the well-being of everyone under their care. Never mind what threats might arise from outside – the Eight will stand fast against them all.

Eights With Other Types

Eights are great at protecting the weak and standing up for what's fair, but that doesn't provide much conflict for an author. Instead, take a look at what can go wrong when a Eight encounters any of the nine types.

Eight & One

Both have strong feelings, but One cares more about public opinion than Eight. "Knock it off, One, you're too judgmental."

"Well, if you'd look at yourself you'd see I'm right." "You *always* think you're right." "I always am."

Eight & Two

"Oh, dear," sighs Two, "you hurt someone's feelings at the party." "Come on, I was just being myself," protests Eight. "Eight, you know how much I love you, so why do you always make things hard for me?" "Why do you always sigh at me?"

Eight & Three

"Let's do it this way." "No, this way." "My way is better." "No, my way is better." "The whole point is, don't you want to be the best?" "Yes, that's why we need to do it this way." "No, that's why we need to do it *my* way."

Eight & Four

An intense relationship, because both feel like they're above the rules. Eight admires and envies Four's artistic creativity, Four admires and envies Eight's emotional authenticity. But when they're angry, the sparks fly!

Eight & Five

"Okay, Five, you need to pick up the delivery by six." "I'll try and remember." "You won't remember unless I remind you, right?" "Well, you're so good at organizing things…" "But why can't I ever count on you for backup?"

Eight & Six

Eight prefers rushing into action against any perceived opposition, while Six considers every possible danger. "You haven't thought this through!" "If I waited for you to analyze every single risk, we'd still be sitting here next year."

Eight & Seven

Eight won't put up with Seven's attempt to avoid confrontations with charm, and Seven won't put up with Eight's anger. "We need to sit down and talk about this." "Maybe tomorrow." "No, right now." "So long, I'm outta here."

Eight & Eight

Each of them knows there's only one best way to do things. Each one knows the other is flat-out wrong. Neither one sees any reason to give in and let the other person take control. Why should they share power with someone else?

Eight & Nine

"Are you mad at me?" asks Eight. Nine doesn't reply. "Just because I yelled about the car?" Nine shrugs and stays quiet. "Look, if you won't speak up, how can we get anything settled?" "You never listen to me anyway," Nine mutters.

You see how none of these is a life-and-death conflict? But each one can be intensified or relieved, depending on where you are in the story.

Some conflicts may strike you as overly dramatic or overly boring. That's okay. That's a clear sign that your story doesn't *need* such a conflict. You may have enough conflict already. If you do need more, though, it's a safe bet that at least one of these examples will spark some ideas. And that's where the fun begins.

Scenarios With Eights

No matter what kind of story you're telling, the characters' personality types will make a difference in the conflict that arises. Here are examples of five stories – about a detective, a princess, a cowboy, a teenager and a career woman – where the protagonist will come into conflict because of his or her enneagram type.

= = = = = = = =

Let's start with the cop trying to track down a blackmailer who's threatening the arrogant father-in-law of his beloved daughter. Jack Warner is a Eight, and he couldn't be happier with his work. This is life at its most intense, going head-to-head with the bad guys. With anybody who's dumb enough or conceited enough to think they can put something over on Jack Warner.

Too bad Karen's father-in-law is such a jerk, but even so the guy deserves police protection. And Jack's just the man to provide it. He'll call in the financial team, figure out where this money is moving, and make the arrest himself. Kane and Taylor might want to horn in, but this is Jack's case. He's gonna show his daughter what a good cop can do.

Only problem is, there's not a whole lot *to* do. The blackmailer has left a trail a mile wide, and the only task is to show up at the bank next Monday and nail the guy. Not much of a challenge there. Maybe the blackmailer will resist arrest, which could make things a little more exciting, but even so Monday looks like a pretty dull day.

So it catches Jack by surprise when the bank clerk signals that the person at the far window is the one he's been waiting for. This looks like a teenage girl, and he didn't come here to take down a teenage girl. Yeah, she's got the marked check – but does that mean the blackmailer is enlisting kids to do his dirty work?

Well, if that's the case, he's in for more trouble than ever. Jack won't stand for somebody using kids, and he'll do whatever he can to help this girl who's crying about her baby-sitting money. Call in Social Services, buy her a chocolate shake, whatever it'll take to make her stop crying. This isn't even his department, but he's not gonna leave this poor kid by herself while they wait for somebody to show up.

Once she's taken care of, he's *really* ready for action. So the blackmailer thought he could put something over on Jack Warner? Not gonna happen. This is gonna be a fight to the death – or at least until one of them winds up behind bars, and Jack won't let that one be himself.

Now this story could move in a lot of different directions.

Maybe Jack will go too far in pursuing the blackmailer, and wind up accused of a crime. Maybe he'll keep checking back on that poor babysitter and discover a whole new case. Maybe Kane and Taylor will convince him he can't do it all himself.

Your character. Your call.

= = = = = = = =

Next comes the princess trying to choose the best ally to defend her kingdom from an invasion of trolls – either the renegade dragon-rider, or the vampire lord.

As an Eight, Aliana will do whatever she can to protect her people. But why does it have to involve a choice like this?

Kelwyn's all right – the dragon-rider doesn't believe in putting on a facade any more than she does – but he'll demand half the kingdom in exchange for his help. And while Varek won't insist on sharing her territory, she can't stand how the vampire lord is always so determined to stick to his ludicrous rules of behavior.

Still, maybe she can put up with that if it means keeping the kingdom intact. She'll go ahead and wear the right jewels, observe all the rituals decreed by that annoying lord, and see if she can't convince him by sheer force of will that he needs to help defend the castle. It's a waste of time, acting like she *believes* those social niceties Varek insists on, but it's still better than sharing her land with Kelwyn.

But putting on a show irritates her, and when Varek refuses to help, she vows to take revenge as soon as the trolls are repelled. He can't expect her to overlook this entire episode, and she wouldn't respect herself if she did.

Meanwhile, she'll have to see what kind of arrangement she can work out with Kelwyn.

Because giving up half the kingdom is unacceptable. She can't live with that. Maybe a quarter, if he'll settle for that land out beyond the swamp. It'll mean uprooting some peasants, but that's still better than letting the entire kingdom be overrun.

So all right. It's a relief to throw off the jewels she wore for Varek, and get back into her riding clothes. Off to convince the dragon-rider that he'll be better off keeping her as a friend than an enemy, and that the swamp is a great place for training young dragons.

But Kelwyn catches her off guard when he volunteers his help without mentioning repayment. That sounds too good to be true, and sure enough, it is. Because just as she's ready to accept his offer, he mentions that of course it's based on her becoming his wife.

Oh, no. No. Aliana knows what it means to marry – it's a total loss of freedom. Even though his lack of royal blood would mean she's still in charge of the kingdom, she doesn't want a husband setting her schedule. Making demands. No, there has to be some other way.

But what?

= = = = = = = =

Now, here's our cowboy facing off against the cattle rustlers. Buck is an Eight, so he's well equipped for battle. Not just the six-gun on his hip and the rifle in his saddlebag, but he's never been one to back down from a fight. Anytime somebody tries to mess with Buck or anyone else on the Triple C, he's ready to set them straight.

So these rustlers are really asking for trouble, and Buck's just the man to give it to 'em. Let 'em come. He can take two or three single-handed, he feels pretty certain, but there's no use telling the other cowboys to stay back at the bunkhouse.

They want to do their part, and Buck appreciates that kind of loyalty. Not like he needs a whole lot of backup, but he might as well let 'em come along.

Still, he knows – even if the other hands have never stopped to figure it out – that the most dangerous job is riding at the front of the posse. So of course Buck will take that position himself.

He wouldn't ask anyone to do a job he's afraid of, and the good Lord knows he *isn't* afraid. Never has been. Never will be. Fear? Ha! Buck doesn't know the meaning of the word. Anybody ever tries to call him a coward, and he'll set them straight in no time.

Besides, it ain't like there's much to be afraid of. A few sorry rustlers, so what? Riding point is the best place to be, because as long as Buck sees them before they see him, the battle will be over in no time at all.

Yep. Nothing to worry about. Except maybe Jeb.

Not like he's afraid of Jeb, either.

It's just, that cowboy never seems to say exactly what he's thinking. Saddling up tonight, he was muttering something about rustlers at the Triple D, and how they made off with the foreman's pony before anyone fired a shot. How things might not be as simple as they look.

Buck isn't so sure he wants Jeb guarding his right, but he's not gonna say *that*. Because that'd make it sound like he's scared, which of course he isn't. Not him. No sir. Matter of fact, he oughta just *ask* Jeb what's going on. No pussy-footing around. What happened at the Triple D? Simple question, simple answer. What's to be scared of?

He ain't scared. Not him. Not Buck. He can shoot the head off a nail at forty paces, and anybody who says otherwise doesn't know what they're talking about. So bring on those rustlers, right now. Come on. Come on. Come on!

= = = = = = = =

Let's take a look at the teenager whose only friend finds a buried treasure in the family's backyard.

Jamie is an Eight, which means that having to take orders from anyone is a royal pain. Kelly knows better than to try bossing Jamie around, but with this treasure there'll be all kinds of people sticking their two cents in. And that's the last thing Jamie wants.

It's a safe bet, though, that Dad's gonna talk about filling out a police report. Mom's gonna get all worried about tax ramifications. Why do people always have to make such a big deal about things, anyway? Why can't they just say "great, a treasure" and let it go at that?

But nobody ever sees things the way Jamie does. Especially not Mom and Dad, who keep making up rules just for the fun of it. Sure, it's all presented under the guise of "wanting you to be safe," but Jamie knows better. It's really about being in charge.

So maybe the smart thing to do is to keep quiet about this discovery. Convince Kelly that they need to handle it by themselves, not drag in anyone else. See what they can get at the pawn shop in town before making the big announcement. Then it'll be too late for people to start throwing rules around – they'll already have the cash in hand.

Saving some of it for college is okay; Jamie's got no problem with that. That's the kind of rule that makes sense, it's not just something Mom and Dad came up with because they like making people jump through hoops. It's not like Jamie minds listening to rules if there's some good reason for 'em. But way too often, there isn't.

All right, then. Time to explain things to Kelly, figure out how to keep things quiet until they can make it to the pawn shop. Maybe get a ride from someone at school who won't blurt everything out the minute anyone asks.

Jamie's been accused of blurting things out, but there's a difference. If someone *asks* you to keep a secret, you keep it. Otherwise, it's too much trouble remembering who's not supposed to know what.

People have too many secrets, anyway, as far as Jamie is concerned. Kelly doesn't want anyone to know about some childhood heart murmur, and that's fine, but most secrets are just stupid. People trying to feel like they're important, when the fact is they're pretty ordinary.

Even Jamie is ordinary, some of the time. But not anymore. This treasure is going to mean freedom, getting some control over things like who picks the college. This treasure will make all the difference.

= = = = = = = =

Finally, the career woman who hires a detective to find the baby she gave up for adoption 13 years ago. As a Eight, Anne might have had any number of reasons for the adoption – let's say she knew the child deserved to grow up with people who were ready to be parents, not with a girl who hadn't even finished high school.

But now she's discovered some rare disease which the adoptive parents must be warned about, and clearly the right thing to do is to notify the family.

She doesn't know where they are, but a detective should be able to track them down. Anne gives Craig all the paperwork she's got, and sends him on his way.

It startles her when he returns with the news that Emily and her adoptive parents would love to meet Anne in person. She isn't so sure – what can she *say* to these people? – but she hates to disappoint a 13-year-old girl. How hard can it be, anyway, taking a few days off and flying across the country?

Okay, she can do this. Piece of cake. Craig says he's coming with her, which she decides might be enjoyable, but of course she doesn't *need* him along.

She's completely unprepared for the rush of emotion that attacks her when she first sees Emily. For some reason she's caught off guard by this younger, more innocent version of herself…before she made the mistake of trusting the boy who left her pregnant.

Isn't there some kind of advice she should offer? Some kind of wisdom she should pass along?

The question haunts her all the way home, and she winds up crying – worse yet, in front of Craig. It's not like she needs him taking care of her, Anne knows, but it's kind of a nice change to let someone else handle the boarding passes and summon a cab.

Still, when the man suggests keeping in touch, she hesitates. Relationships aren't her strong point, and there's no point hoping for any kind of a future with a man who's seen her at her weakest moment.

But Craig won't take no for an answer. He says he'll give her all the time she needs to get used to the idea, but he's not walking out of her life. Which is both promising and disturbing, because how does she know she can trust him?

Sure, *he* offered her a shoulder to cry on, but that's a far cry from *her* offering him her love. Just because he's seen her softer side doesn't mean he really cares. Maybe she'd like having him in her life...but what if she can't control the situation and he winds up stomping on her heart?

Keep in mind that even if she decides to trust Craig with her heart, she's still an Eight. A happier, healthier Eight who's overcome the fatal flaw of lust – lust for power over every aspect of life – but an Eight nonetheless.

Nobody changes their type. They can change their outlook on life, they can change the traits which have kept them from being the best they can be, but their fundamental type never changes.

Because remember how all nine types can be terrific people? A happy ending just means that this particular type has found their best self. A tragic ending means they've found it and turned away. An either-way ending means they haven't found it yet...but maybe they will in the next story.

You're the writer. You can pick. And readers who share your view of the world will be delighted with whatever choice you make.

CHAPTER NINE

QUIZ

- ☐ Do you figure most things in life aren't worth getting upset about?
- ☐ Are you generally relaxed and comfortable?
- ☐ Is it hard for you to make choices?
- ☐ Do people see you as affable, easygoing and peace-loving?
- ☐ Do you tend to procrastinate?
- ☐ Is personal comfort important to you?
- ☐ Do other people's confrontations make you uncomfortable?
- ☐ Are you fairly attached to your habits and schedules?
- ☐ Do you generally feel at one with nature and other people?
- ☐ Are you good at promoting harmony and unity?

___ **TOTAL FOR NINE**

TYPE NINE:
The Peacemaker, The Mediator

Nines want the world to be at peace. So do most people, but tranquility and harmony and unity matter more to a Nine than to any other type.

If Nines could always be at one with the people around them, at one with the world around them and with the very air around them, they'd be perfectly happy. They like it when everyone gets along, when there's no conflict anywhere, and nobody has to take sides.

Taking sides is something a Nine would rather avoid. Even picking chocolate or vanilla can become a tough choice when it's so easy to see the advantages of every possible option.

Nines are great at seeing the advantages of any and every decision, so they can make a good case for whatever course of action anyone suggests.

This makes them natural diplomats, because they can identify with so many viewpoints that everyone around them feels understood. No wonder they become known among their friends as the ideal mediator, the one everybody finds it easy to get along with.

Getting along with everyone is part of Nines' essential makeup, and the only disadvantage of such skill is that identifying so strongly with others may keep them from developing their personal self.

Those who *do* recognize their own needs and desires, along with the needs and desires of whomever is nearby, are better able to deal with conflict when it arises. Even so, they'd prefer to have things peaceful. Aggression is something they'd rather not deal with – even if it comes from within. So when Nines start feeling annoyed or angry, they may take that as their cue to simply shut down.

Nines can stay shut down for long periods of time, and on the surface no one would ever notice. They'll stay busy and active, but their activity may not be prompted by genuine passion or drive. It might just be a way to avoid dealing with problems. "I can't face off against the unfair boss right now, because I have to pick up some envelopes and put gas in the car and stop by the bank and remind Mom about the vitamins."

Anyone hoping to face off against a Nine for a heart-to-heart confrontation will be in for a long wait.

But that same quality makes them enjoyable companions, because they'll always accept you as you are. Some might call it a peace-at-any-price mentality; others might call it non-judgmental, even-tempered or easygoing. Either way, Nines tend to be very open-minded and relaxed, the type who's enjoyable to have around under almost any circumstances.

The most well-adjusted Nines are completely comfortable with every facet of themselves and with everyone around them. They don't see any need to put on airs, to control other people, to acquire more than they already have.

Instead they simply enjoy whatever unfolds before them, allowing plenty of time to relax in comfortable serenity.

Meanwhile, though, the less well-adjusted Nines are working tirelessly to become one with whomever is nearby at the moment – either ignoring or flat-out denying any personal feelings, desires and ideas that might shake up the status quo. They'll divert themselves with trivia instead, and decline to make decisions on their own.

Rather than disagree with any situation, they'll simply retreat. If all the neighbors are planning a party for Friday night and a couple of Nines don't want to attend, nobody will ever hear them say "no." But on Friday night, there won't be any sign of the Nines…and everyone will be surprised. "Didn't they say they were coming?"

Well, no. They probably sat through the planning sessions looking pleasant – no point in disturbing the happy energy of the group – and not committing one way or another.

But when they *do* attend the next party, everyone will go home raving about what great people those Nines are. Wonderful listeners. So easy to be with. Incredibly diplomatic. Always ready to lend a hand or share a good story or make you feel understood. What's not to love about a Nine?

Famous Nines

Because Nines are so good at adapting to whatever the circumstances require, it can be hard to pick them out of a crowd. If they're surrounded by Twos, they'll take on the traits of a Two. If they're mixing with Fives, they'll seem like Fives. They're great at fitting in.

You can see that characteristic in people who've spent a lot of time in the public eye. Look at Queen Elizabeth, Ronald Reagan or Dwight Eisenhower. Regardless of how you might feel about them politically, it'd be hard to feel personally offended by any of them.

Look at Jimmy Stewart. Nice guy, what's not to like? Look at Grace Kelly. Same thing. Gary Cooper. Nines are the kind of people anyone would be happy to sit next to in a crowd.

They're pleasantly accommodating and easy to get along with, not the type to make you feel threatened or uneasy or inferior. Instead, you'll leave a conversation with them feeling honored, appreciated and understood.

Maybe everyone else in the group is running around trying to make order out of chaos, but the Nine is curiously undisturbed. A good example would be Jerry Seinfeld, whose fellow TV characters went through all kinds of ups and downs during any given season…while he simply let all the drama unfold.

When Nines turn their attention to helping others, it's always in a more low-key way than a loud and brassy way. Look at Audrey Hepburn raising money to fight hunger. Look at Carl Jung exploring the depths of the mind. Look at Norman Rockwell painting scenes that reflect the peaceful life so many people dream of. No matter what arena they work in, Nines have a gift for making people feel comfortable and secure.

Nine's Heroic Strengths

A Nine is great at understanding how you feel, at finding common ground among everyone in the room, and at keeping things calm with a relaxing demeanor. They don't carry grudges, they don't scheme for power, they don't look for hidden flaws. They look on the bright side, and they bring out the best in other people.

How do they manage that? It's because they're so good at identifying with others.

They offer wholehearted acceptance and a remarkable lack of criticism. They don't make demands. They take you exactly as you are, value you for who you are, and that's a rare gift.

It's been said that more women want to marry Nines than any other types, and you can see why that's likely. Nines tend to be consistently pleasant, patient, empathetic and easygoing. They appreciate the small wonders that most people take for granted, often showing an almost childlike delight in the beauty of a sunny sky or the satisfying crunch of an apple.

This same innocence gives them an open-minded quality – they'll never rush to judgment over anything. Someone who's unaffected by personal ego, pretense or competition is always at ease among friends and strangers alike, and perfectly willing to serve as a solid anchor of tranquility amidst any chaos.

People might take Nines for granted, but they'll never hear a Nine complain about it.

The best Nines are as comfortable with their own feelings as they are with everyone else's, and fully involved in the present moment. They can put up with stress and annoyance, viewing it in a wider perspective, which lets them stay relaxed no matter what happens around them.

Anytime you see someone sitting back and smiling at the surroundings without jumping in to change things around, it's likely you've spotted a Nine.

Nine's Fatal Flaws

The very easygoing nature that makes Nines so appealing can also make them hard to live with. Being relaxed is one side of the coin, but refusing to get involved can be carried to extremes – at which point you might find the Nine lazing by the TV with piles of bills and dirty dishes stacked everywhere, convinced that "everything will turn out just fine."

It adds up to a picture of sloth, which is Nine's fatal flaw. Most Nines will turn off the TV and wash some dishes before food poisoning sets in, but there's always the inclination to just take things easy. Not necessarily in the physical sense, although Nines make wonderful couch potatoes, but also in the emotional sense of refusing to acknowledge any problems in life.

Nines are good at compartmentalizing their lives, moving from home to work to the grocery store to the volunteer fire department to the neighbors' barbecue to the co-worker's wedding without ever becoming fully engaged in any of those events. They'll go through the motions just fine, but their feelings are somewhere else...floating beyond reach.

Why should they get in touch with feelings which might be unpleasant? Better to just enjoy the soft quilt at home, the hot coffee at the fire station, the friendly chatter at the barbecue, than to open up to any possible problem.

Just relax, just stay calm, just smile at everyone and move along to the next stop.

So the only way for a Nine to overcome the habit of sloth is to actively take a stand – "Here's what I believe, here's what I want, and here's what I'm going to do about it." It's a dramatic turnaround, and the beginning of a whole new life for the formerly un-involved Nine.

Nines As Children

Naturally, little Nines like everything to stay pleasant. They're upset by clashes at home or at school; they want everyone to get along. And if anyone nearby is arguing, they're likely to either tune it out or step in and try to make peace.

If something annoys them, they're likely to tune *that* out as well. They'll focus instead on something pleasant and comfortable, like watching TV or eating potato chips or curling up with their favorite blanket.

Nines are very attuned to sensual pleasures, and they actively enjoy those pleasures – sometimes to the point of addiction, but often simply as a satisfying substitute for engaging in any kind of conflict.

Getting mad or upset can create conflict, so Nines will try to avoid that and usually wind up with a reputation as "good" children. But they can surprise everyone with an occasional angry outburst or show of rebellion, which is a sign that they haven't completely denied their own feelings.

Parents who encourage their young Nines to stand up for themselves are doing them a huge favor, because Nines don't usually take time to identify their own desires.

Part of that is because they see so many options and hate to decide on just one, but part is because they hate to make a fuss about anything. Both those characteristics – seeing numerous options and preferring to avoid conflict – make them wonderful mediators among their friends.

In fact, while they're not usually social leaders, Nines are popular with other children. Just like their adult counterparts, they're easy to get along with, good at accepting others and good at working out solutions, which makes them a valued part of any group.

Nines At Work

At work, Nines are good for the long haul. Any job that requires maintaining a comfortable status quo is perfect for their amiable style, whether it involves working with people or ideas or mechanics or trees. They'll fit easily into whatever environment surrounds them, settling happily into a familiar routine.

If there are decisions to be made, the Nine would just as soon let someone else do it. If there's recognition to be awarded, the Nine wouldn't mind having some – but will never ask for it. If there's any opportunity for self-promotion, the Nine will step gingerly around it. Let somebody else get the credit.

The only thing worse than having to make decisions is having to face surprises. When unexpected events happen at work, Nines tend to feel overwhelmed. How can they tell whether it's more important to rescue the secretary or the receptionist? Everything and everyone around them seems equally important, which makes it impossible to decide on a course of action.

Non-action is how Nines control their environment. They might look wonderfully efficient, zipping through tasks at high speed, but they're working on "automatic" most of the time.

They know what has to be done and how to do it, so why look for trouble? Just keep going, and everything will be fine. Just fine.

Because they want to avoid conflict wherever possible, they'd rather not be pinned down on any question. Broad, generic goals like "make the world a better place" are far more appealing than specific goals which might raise controversial issues.

Better to keep things smooth. Better to get along with everyone. Better to be a good listener, help mediate so all sides feel understood, and let everything work out fine. Just fine.

Nines In Relationships

As easy as they are to get along with, Nines can be tough when it comes to commitment. They might go through all the motions, but never become fully involved in the relationship… instead taking refuge in comfortable habits and trivial pursuits rather than genuine intimacy.

A Nine who refuses to get involved might be considered passive-aggressive, in that anyone who *wants* some interaction will have to work to get it. After all, it's hard to interact with someone who just smiles and floats along.

But it's usually easy to enjoy someone who's consistently kind and gentle, loyal and supportive, reassuring and nonjudgmental. Nines give off a sense of cozy comfort that's tremendously appealing, as long as you don't want anything more.

Well-adjusted Nines are those who can acknowledge and maintain their own preferences while maintaining close relationships as well. But others might hide their true selves and instead "merge" with others, simply echoing their friends' beliefs and wishes rather than expressing any of their own.

This can become a habit, and a Nine who's used to repressing personal feelings in favor of a partner's feelings will have a tough time changing. They might assert themselves by refusing to take action, in a classic passive-aggressive style where whoever cares least is the one who wins.

Encouraging such Nines to clarify their own desires, sometimes offering choices which can't be answered with "whichever *you* want," can help them learn to acknowledge and express their feelings. They might never have learned to mention that they want to be alone, and deciding what they don't want (as well as what they do) can help Nines take ownership of their feelings – at which point, they become virtually ideal mates.

Nine's Individual Subtype

Nines value physical comfort no matter what their subtype, but as you can imagine, they value it even more with the self-preservation type. Maintaining their comfortable habits is as important as satisfying their current appetites, and they'll devote more attention to such maintenance than to just about anything else.

Of course, if they wind up facing off against someone else at the grocery store when they both want the last bag of potato chips, the self-preservation Nine will be in a dilemma. Which is worse, conflict or no potato chips? But if there's a bag of corn chips two feet away, everything will be just fine.

While friends and neighbors might view this Nine as a couch potato, the Nine sure doesn't *feel* lazy. It takes some effort to make sure the cable TV bill is paid every month, that the refrigerator never runs out of drinks, and that the sofa cushions stay at just the right angle for maximum comfort. That's what life is about!

Or if it's not about the couch, it's about collecting a favorite item. Repeating a favorite trip. Preparing a favorite recipe. Why risk a new recipe when the old one is always great? Why travel somewhere else when the old place is so pleasant? Why look for something different in life when everything is so comfortable the way it is now?

Nine's Intimacy Subtype

What matters most to an intimacy-subtype person is, clearly, relationships. For a Nine, that relationship may be the dream of some ideal romantic union that keeps them yearning for the perfect mate, constantly searching for just the right person who will make life complete.

If that person is already sharing their kitchen and bedroom, the Nine may be tempted to deny any flaws. "I already have the perfect mate, and our life is utterly happy. Who cares about the lid off the toothpaste, the bounced checks, the mysterious emails? Why question perfection?"

That way, there's no risk of discovering that the relationship may need work. With an Ideal Mate, there's no need to look for any other purpose in life – a purpose which might involve making some new and difficult effort or commitment. A Great Relationship already at hand is enough of a purpose in life.

A relationship-subtype Nine who doesn't have such a mate handy will keep looking for someone to idealize. Being able to lose oneself in the quest for a mate, or in the sheer "don't tell *me* about any flaws" perfection of the mate at hand, lets these Nines immerse themselves in their vision of the consummate relationship and shut out any other pesky little details of life.

Nine's Social Subtype

Nines who value the welfare of their society above all else are good at playing along. They're skilled at fitting into whatever role will make things easy for themselves and everyone around them.

But if the group starts making demands – "you have to be here every Thursday" – the Nine will resist. Very amiably, very gently, to the point where nobody will ever complain, but effectively enough that the group will come to understand they can't expect to see the Nine every Thursday.

In fact, a Nine who's involved with any society faces constant ambivalence. They enjoy being part of the group, because it lets them feel included and loved. Even better, it lets them get by with minimal participation, since showing up every once in a while to stuff envelopes isn't really much of a commitment and it keeps everyone feeling good.

But deep inside, this Nine may resent the fact that "the group doesn't really *see* me for who I am. Sure, it's a fun place to hang out, but I can't be all things to all people." And yet it's that very ability to be all things to all people which makes the Nine so popular.

While a societal-subtype Nine may avoid showing companions anything beyond a pleasant facade, those who do take such a risk become even more highly valued members of the group.

Nines With Other Types

Nines are great at seeing all sides of a question and keeping the peace, but that doesn't provide much conflict for an author. Instead, take a look at what can go wrong when a Nine encounters any of the nine types.

Nine & One

Nine just wants to relax, while One has a plan for the day. "Relaxing is fine in its place, but we need to get things straightened out." "You can handle it without me." "But that's not fair." Nine shrugs. One fumes. Nine retreats…

Nine & Two

Two wants to talk about a problem between them. Nine would rather withdraw. Two cries, “I need interaction.” Nine goes to another room and shuts the door. Two feels neglected and ignored. Nine feels invaded and pursued.

Nine & Three

Three wants Nine’s opinion on a new first-day-on-the-job suit. “Looks fine to me,” says Nine. “No, come on, this is important.” “I said it looked fine.” “You’re not really concentrating. Don’t you understand how important this is?”

Nine & Four

Four wants Nine to be fully involved. “I *am* involved; I’m right here in the room with you.” “But you’re not showing me your deepest self.” “I can’t ever make you happy.” “You could at least *try*.” “It’ll never be enough for you.”

Nine & Five

“Hey, Nine, listen to this great research proposal.” “Oh, my show’s on – but okay, go ahead.” “No, if you’d rather watch your show, I guess that’s more important.” “I said, go ahead!” “Never mind, you’ll resent every minute of it.”

Nine & Six

They’re both slow to action. “You talk first,” says Six. “No, *you* go first.” “I need to think about it.” “No rush,” says Nine, leaning back more comfortably. “Aren’t you giving any thought to what *could* happen?” “Nope. Here, you go first.”

Nine & Seven

“So many options,” says Seven. “I know,” Nine agrees, “what should we pick?” “This might be good, but so might that.” “Or that, or that….” “Well, let’s quit pondering and *do* something.” “You’re always pushing me,” says Nine.

Nine & Eight

"Are you mad at me?" asks Eight. Nine doesn't reply. "Just because I yelled about the car?" Nine shrugs and stays quiet. "Look, if you won't speak up, how can we get anything settled?" "You never listen to me anyway," Nine mutters.

Nine & Nine

No need to deal with issues. No need to confront problems. No need to worry if the car has another flat tire; things will work out just fine by themselves. Eventually both Nines will be in a flat-tired car, telling themselves it'll be okay.

You see how none of these is a life-and-death conflict? (Well, unless the car is stuck in the Sahara Desert....) But each one can be intensified or relieved, depending on where you are in the story.

Some conflicts may strike you as overly dramatic or overly boring. That's okay. That's a clear sign that your story doesn't *need* such a conflict. You may have enough conflict already. If you do need more, though, it's a safe bet that at least one of these examples will spark some ideas. And that's where the fun begins.

Scenarios With Nines

No matter what kind of story you're telling, the characters' personality types will make a difference in the conflict that arises. Here are examples of five stories – about a detective, a princess, a cowboy, a teenager and a career woman – where the protagonist will come into conflict because of his or her enneagram type.

= = = = = = = =

Let's start with the cop trying to track down a blackmailer who's threatening the arrogant father-in-law of his beloved daughter. Jack Warner is a Nine, although it's hard to imagine how someone who dislikes conflict became a cop in the first place. Police work must be a family tradition – if Dad and Grandpa and Uncle Mike were all on the force, Jack wouldn't want to drop the ball.

Anyway, he's great when it comes to community relations, teaching schoolchildren that cops are on their side, and reassuring little old ladies that their lost cat will be found in no time. So now he's comfortably immersed in his daily routine of dropping by schools, taking reports and making newly arrested suspects feel like *here's* someone they can talk to, when he gets a call from his daughter.

Karen needs help, and there's no way Jack can ignore that. His first inclination might be to wait and see if perhaps things will settle down without any intervention, but when she explains that the blackmailer's threats are increasing, he knows it's time to take action.

All right, then. He'll investigate. Talk to whoever might have some information – after all, he's great at that – and see if he can't just get this whole thing settled without a whole lot of angst.

Problem is, he can't. (If he could, we wouldn't have a story.) No, instead he's faced with the fact that skillful negotiating won't solve this case. He's going to have to crack down, make some demands, and already the idea has him twisted in knots.

Maybe Taylor could handle this? After all, Jack still has to pick up the school posters, put gas in the patrol car, make sure his badge is shined, assure Karen things will turn out fine – his day is more than full as it *is*, so how can he possibly catch a blackmailer on top of everything else?

But suppose the evidence winds up on his desk, in full view of the entire squad.

Suppose Taylor has already told everyone it was Jack who interviewed the witnesses, and Jack who deserves to make the arrest.

Is he supposed to stand up in front of the whole department and insist that someone else take over? How would Karen feel about that? Will Captain Ryan be disappointed? No matter what he does, things are going to get sticky, and there doesn't seem to be any way out of this.

Maybe he'll go for a burger and spend three hours staring at the TV above the bar. Maybe he'll muster up the determination to get the job done, or to officially turn it down. It's your story… and Jack's.

= = = = = = = = =

Next comes the princess trying to choose the best ally to defend her kingdom from an invasion of trolls – either the renegade dragon-rider, or the vampire lord.

As a Nine, Aliana has done a superlative job of keeping the two enemies at bay. Each one feels like she's on *his* side, and while she's never attempted to invite them both to dinner on the same night, she's managed to avoid any clashes so far.

But now, with the trolls advancing, she knows she'll have to make a choice. Kelwyn is all in favor of launching a dragon attack against the invaders, while Varek insists that draining their blood is the only possible solution, and Aliana can no longer placate them both with pleasant, generic promises. She has to enlist an ally, and she has to do it fast.

How to accomplish that? Enlisting an ally is no problem, of course, because every neighbor of her kingdom is willing to swear loyalty to the princess who always listens and never judges. But she can't choose both men to help her repel the invaders, because they'll clash so fiercely that her peasants will wind up scorched by dragon fire *and* missing all their blood. No, inviting both Varek and Kelwyn to help fight her battle would be worse than doing nothing at all.

Doing nothing at all. Hmm.

Is it possible that this is all just a tempest in a teapot? Is it possible that the reports of invasion are exaggerated? Why, maybe she's been worrying needlessly all this time! Maybe she just needs a quiet stroll by the lake, and everything will turn out fine.

But here comes another peasant, with news that the trolls are only a day's march away. And her maid with a note from Varek, announcing that he's bringing his vampires to assist her. And a courtier with word from Kelwyn that he'll arrive within the hour.

Well, Aliana decides, right now the most important thing is to choose the proper flowers for tonight's banquet. The tulips are unusually bright this year, and the gardeners have done wonders with the roses. The vampires will appreciate blood-red centerpieces, and the tulips bear a striking resemblance to the dragon-rider's shield…

"No need to worry," she tells her maid, who seems dreadfully upset about something or other. "Let's get these flowers picked, shall we?"

That doesn't seem to placate the maid, and Aliana sighs. Why do people insist on making a big deal out of every little problem? With all these lovely flowers surrounding them, why can't they just enjoy the beauty of the moment?

= = = = = = = =

Now, here's our cowboy facing off against the cattle rustlers. Buck is a Nine, and ranch life has been good to him.

There's always a warm stove on a winter's night, plenty of solitude when he feels like being alone, and company in the bunkhouse when he feels like shooting the breeze.

Better yet, the new schoolmarm in town is the most beautiful woman he's ever laid eyes on, and last week she smiled at him after church.

Yes, life is good…except for those pesky rustlers who seem bent on nabbing cattle from the Triple C. Buck has drawn the first watch, and so far there's no sign of trouble. If he spots any rustlers, though, all he has to do is sound the alarm and the other cowboys will come running.

For now, though, it's just himself and the campfire. And the longer he gazes at the flames, the easier it is to see Miss Lillian's smile.

Glowing, kind of, the way she looked outside the Trout Creek Church last Sunday. The kind of woman he could spend a lifetime loving, although he knows better than to say anything like that to a lady like her.

No, with a lady you need to watch what you say. Don't be too bold. Frenchy over at the Triple D tried that once, with the new saloon gal, and look how *that* turned out. Beer everywhere. Buck ain't gonna make a mistake like that.

Because Miss Lillian deserves better. She deserves the kind of fellow who'll give her jewels the size of hens' eggs, not just blather on about how beautiful she is. Buck's gonna save up for a brooch or something, the kind of gift he can give a lady like her, because once she knows how he feels about her…well, life's good right now, but with her it can only get better.

She's from Missouri, he's pretty certain, and he'll happily follow her back to Missouri. Or Wyoming. Wherever she wants to go. Buck's got no preference, he likes the Triple C fine but it's more important that Miss Lillian be happy with wherever they live.

And if she – wait a minute, is that someone sneaking past the gate? Yeah, gotta sound the alarm. No question there. Easy decision, no need to think about it. That's the kind of decision Buck likes.

Yep, here come the other cowboys. Time to set the rustlers straight. Once this is done, though, it's a safe bet he'll wind up with some reward money. Enough to pick out something special for Miss Lillian. Or maybe wait a while. Think it over. No need to rush into anything hasty…

= = = = = = = =

Let's take a look at the teenager whose only friend finds a buried treasure in the family's backyard.

Jamie is a Nine, which makes it unusual that there's only one friend in the picture. But let's say the family just moved here, school hasn't started yet, and nobody lives nearby except Kelly.

Which is fine. Jamie likes Kelly, it's good having someone to swim with, someone to get nachos with. Someone who doesn't mind helping out when Mom needs the garden weeded, which is a lot bigger job than they expected. But it's a job that wound up yielding this out-of-nowhere treasure, so Jamie's not about to complain.

Kelly, though, is going crazy with plans – call somebody at the newspaper, wait till everyone at school hears about this – which has Jamie feeling a little uneasy. They might not be entitled to keep anything, so maybe they should wait until Dad hears back from the lawyer before they start spreading the news all over town.

But it's too late to stop Kelly, and now there are reporters wanting a story about Jamie. How many high school kids uncover something this valuable, anyway? Kelly's more than willing to answer questions, but Jamie doesn't feel right about that either. After all, whose house *is* this?

The problem is, everybody wants something different. Dad wants to get legal advice, Mom wants peace and quiet, Kelly wants lots of attention, and Jamie just wants everyone to get along. Is that asking too much?

Apparently it is, because even though normally it's pretty easy to keep everyone calm, right now feelings are running too high.

"I'd start calling around, but it's really your decision," Dad announces, and Mom agrees. "I'd keep quiet, but you're old enough to decide how you want to handle it." Even Kelly concedes that if the reporters are insisting on an interview with Jamie, "you might as well talk to somebody. I'll tell you what to say." Everybody knows how *they* want to handle things, but what's Jamie supposed to do?

Take a stand? That might be tough, especially with so many conflicting opinions. Let everyone else argue among themselves for a while? The conflict is getting too intense. Just slip away until things cool down? There are reporters all up and down the street. None of the options look too good, but how can Jamie get any space to make decisions with everyone yelling about what they want?

Is it time to stand up and make an announcement? Time to say "here's what *I* want?" Jamie isn't sure…so here's where you come in!

= = = = = = = = =

Finally, the career woman who hires a detective to find the baby she gave up for adoption 13 years ago. As a Nine, Anne might have had any number of reasons for the adoption – let's say her parents preferred not to raise a grandchild, and she was too young to care for a baby on her own.

But now she's discovered some rare disease which the adoptive parents must be warned about, and her secretary's brother has just opened his own detective agency, so Anne agrees to give this curiously attractive man the business of tracking down her birth daughter.

It turns out, though, that Craig isn't the kind of detective who'll make all the decisions on her behalf. Instead he keeps calling her, insisting that she tell him what she wants. Would she rather meet the adoptive parents herself, or have him break the news? Does she want to hear about Emily's life, or refuse any further communication?

Anne tries to evade his questions, the way she does whenever someone asks her opinion, but somehow this man seems to see through her attempts at avoiding a choice. He keeps coming back to the idea of free choice, *her* choice, and insisting she deserves to pick what she wants most.

Finally she tells Craig to break the news himself but to offer a meeting if the parents request it, which they do. Anne is used to taking responsibility for things at work, but this is a whole different mission. How's she going to keep everyone happy, keep everything peaceful, if there are big emotions involved?

Still, Emily is eager to meet her birth mother, and after a month of hesitation – combined with Craig's encouragement to choose what she truly wants – Anne decides that going for a visit will be easier than making more excuses. But when he finally drives her to Emily's house, she shuts down. This is too big to cope with. She can smile politely, say all the right things, but her real self is hiding behind the pleasant facade.

The adoptive family doesn't seem to notice anything wrong, and they even invite her for Emily's birthday party next month, but Anne leaves with no specific promise. Craig calls her on it as soon as they leave. "Either stay involved with her or back out, but don't leave everyone hanging." For the first time in years, she responds with anger…which Craig applauds. "See, you *can* say what you're feeling! Now, how do you feel about having dinner with me?"

Maybe she'll evade the offer. Maybe she'll accept it. Maybe she'll open up a little, then retreat, then take a stand for what she wants.

Keep in mind that even if she lets herself embark on a relationship that involves owning her decisions, she's still a Nine. A happier, healthier Nine who's overcome the fatal flaw of sloth – sitting back and refusing to make any kind of choice – but a Nine nonetheless.

Nobody changes their type. They can change their outlook on life, they can change the traits which have kept them from being the best they can be, but their fundamental type never changes.

Because remember how all nine types can be terrific people? A happy ending just means that this particular type has found their best self. A tragic ending means they've found it and turned away. An either-way ending means they haven't found it yet…but maybe they will in the next story.

You're the writer. You can pick. And readers who share your view of the world will be delighted with whatever choice you make.

CONCLUSION

So that's it. The nine types. What you do with them – as if you didn't know this already – is up to you.

But isn't it wonderful to have so many options?

Now that you've seen the enneagrams and their traits spelled out, you can choose how you want to use them.

Maybe to address new issues within characters you've already created.

Maybe to start from scratch with characters who will likely come into conflict.

Maybe to transform some old characters into new ones with compelling differences.

Regardless of how you use these tools, it's important to remember that believable personalities, flaws and all, need to be set up from the very beginning.

If you like to let your characters develop while you're writing your first draft, that's fine...you can always go back later and adjust their actions, thoughts and feelings to fit the personalities you've created. If you like to have the people's types in place before you start writing, that can make the job easier.

Of course, if you're already happy with a particular story as it is, don't change anything *just* to make your characters match an enneagram type. (Theorists might love you for it, but nobody else will care.)

But if you feel like a character needs some tweaking, then enneagram personalities are a great place to look for inspiration!

Frequently Asked Questions

Whenever I talk about enneagrams in an online class or live workshop, people usually come up with questions similar to those answered below.

If yours are covered here, that's great. If not, let me know – either through the publisher or my www.BookLaurie.com website –

because I'll expand the Q&A session in the next version of this book. And speaking of my website, you'll notice how easy it is to remember when you want to Book Laurie for a workshop!

Flaw Or Strength

Q: Do my characters really *need* flaws? I have a hard time thinking of them as flawed people.

A: A lot of writers, especially those who adore happy endings, feel like people should be fundamentally good. Which makes it hard to view their character traits as flaws.

But in fact, their flaws and their strengths are really two sides of the same coin.

Taking the viewpoint that everybody is doing the best they can with what they've got, it's only logical. Because every single character trait can be tipped toward the bad (for a flaw) or the good (for a strength). It's all in how the character uses a particular trait – and in how those around him or her perceive it.

My mother is a marriage counselor, and her first question to every client is: "What drew you to this person in the first place? Whatever it is, I'll bet it's what's driving you crazy right now."

And it almost always is. Maybe in the beginning Ken loved Barbie's willingness to drop everything and go dancing whenever he could get an evening off work, but after five years together he's annoyed that she'd rather go dancing than spend a relaxing evening at home together.

Maybe at first Barbie loved the way Ken paid such rapturous attention to her, devouring every word she spoke. Now she sees him doing that same thing with everyone, from the paper boy to the elderly couple next door, and resents him conversing so earnestly with strangers when he could be with her instead.

So each of them has a trait which, depending on how you look at it, is either a flaw or a strength.

And since it's all in the perception, don't think of your beloved characters as having flaws. Just think of them as having strengths they need to put into practice!

Mix-and-Match

Q: Can you mix and match personality types within a character?

A: Mix-and-match can be wonderful, because it makes the character even more of a real person than just some sketch lifted out of a Personality Types book.

There might be some types that shouldn't be combined, but I'm having a hard time coming up with any.

At first I was going to say, "You can't have a character who's a stern taskmaster most of the time but who becomes a carefree fun-lover on weekends," then realized that of course you can. Or, "You can't have a character who's afraid of her own shadow most of the time, yet who walks right up to the pirate captain and demands the return of her jewels" – but given the right motivation, you could do that too.

Given the right motivation, you can do just about anything! And if you know that (at some point) your character will do something that might seem strange to most readers, you'll set up the necessary characteristic long before the actual scene.

If the scaredy-cat princess is gonna go after those pirate-held jewels to pay for ransoming her brother, you'll establish right from the start that she's capable of incredibly brave deeds when a loved one is threatened. Problem solved.

It's only when a character's actions or thoughts don't seem to make sense, when it seems like they're a completely different personality than they were in a previous scene, that readers get upset. We've all seen that done. But the problem wasn't that the author combined different personality types – it was that he didn't set it up.

Look at each of us. We're all combinations of dozens of different types – even if all we consider is the enneagram with its Social, Self-Preservation and Intimacy subtypes, the wings on either side and the two other go-to types.

Or in real life, which is usually more interesting than theory: say you're a Democrat, but you admired Ronald Reagan. And you're an agnostic, but you enjoy Midnight Mass. You live in the city but wear country clothes. You love dogs but hate the one next door. Easy to imagine, right? We're all such huge bundles of contradictions that it's perfectly plausible our characters will be, too.

The only difference between us and our characters is that *they* don't have as much scope to reveal all their contradictory facets. In a limited number of pages, we authors have to scale down and show only their most important traits – those which will affect the story.

And that's where it comes in handy to know something about the character's personality…no matter what facets it combines.

So how *do* you learn about the character's personality? Some writers like using tools such as enneagrams. Some like sitting down at the keyboard and seeing what happens. Some prefer chatty or formal interviews. Some create a first-person bio. Some write their first three chapters in a frenzy. Some develop extensive pre-planning charts. There's sure no One Best Way to do this.

But isn't it handy to have a bunch of choices? There's nothing I love more than a full toolbox!

Conflict

Q: How can a character's fatal flaw affect his or her conflict with other people? What about the conflict from within?

A: As we've seen, every personality contains good and bad sides of the same coin. And no matter which side of the coin a trait is on, it's going to affect virtually everything the character does.

But the fatal flaws are especially going to affect a character whenever he's vulnerable – and often when he doesn't even realize he's vulnerable. Great drama, right?

Let's say we've got a Type One character. (Easy to start with #1.) He's got this personality that wants to Do The Right Thing, wants to make sure everyone around him Does The Right Thing, and he'll do whatever it takes to ensure that. But if he fails, if he can't make the Right Thing happen, he's gonna be angry…either at himself, or at the world, or at the specific offender.

Let's say his external conflict is the good old Yankee/ Confederate thing. We'll make him a Southern plantation owner, and say he's faced with a New England volunteer who came to nurse the troops in Georgia.

She wants to use his mansion as a hospital and enlist the remaining field workers as orderlies; he wants to get the crop in so he can pay the taxes that will save the plantation for his loved ones.

Type One John is angry that he can't keep the Yankees from upsetting the entire South, and that anger will spill over when Nurse Mary shows up.

Let's say she's a Two who yearns to be needed, and the idea of being unable to care for her patients sends her into John's dining room crying that he *can't* refuse to help.

External conflict, right?

Not just differing political views, but different views on an immediate situation that anyone in town would agree is a tough decision – whether to save the plantation for a beloved son, or whether to save injured strangers. Both goals are perfectly noble, perfectly understandable, but there's no way these two characters are going to agree.

Now for the internal conflict.

John is beating himself up as it is, fearing that he can't leave Junior the plantation he's loved for a lifetime, and now here's Mary accusing him of utter selfishness. He's torn. His whole life has been about doing the right thing, and yet he can't stop harvesting the crop that'll pay this year's taxes – what's he gonna *do*?

Mary wants to care for people, make them feel better, and yet she sees her tirade making John feel worse. So of course she wants to soothe and nurture *him* as well as her patients, because he needs comforting too. But does he need her as much as they do? Does he need her more? She's torn.

Internal conflict.

And you can do this with any two types you want! Let's take the same scenario, shoot down to the end of the list, and make John a Type Nine and Mary a Type Eight.

So she's trying to get things organized, make things work, start the field hands scrubbing mattress covers, and he's uneasy about the crops beginning to rot out there. He doesn't want to stir up trouble, but he's *got* to get the tobacco harvested. He's torn. He'll suggest a compromise. She'll refuse. He'll point out that the downtrodden sharecroppers need a future as badly as the injured soldiers. She'll be torn. And so on.

Maybe he's a Five who wants to view the situation with analytical detachment, not get emotionally involved, and she's a Six who's jumping in frantically to try and prevent disaster. Again, conflict.

You won't necessarily get such clear-cut conflicts with every possible combination of numbers. (I just got lucky in picking these three scenarios off the top of my head, so don't think you did something wrong if you don't get a winner right off the bat.) But lining up possible conflicts shows how the fatal-flaw premise can enrich *any* story.

Because whether the conflict is internal or external, the character's personality can make it a whole lot more interesting.

The Right Flaws

Q: I want my protagonist to have some flaws, but I don't want him to be overly alpha-male *or* overly wimpy. How do I find the right blend?

A: For illustration purposes: Pick some flaws. Any flaws. In fact, you can pick any of the Seven Deadly Sins and they'll do just fine. Say, anger and greed and sloth.

Now let's build a super-alpha hero who's angry, greedy and slothful. You can picture how he'll act, right? He'll yell at the driver in the next lane for braking too fast. He'll elbow every competitor out of the way to get the biggest sandwich for himself. He'll let six weeks of dirty dishes pile up around him when his girlfriend's out of town and rant about it, rather than hunt down the dishwasher himself.

How will a wimpy guy handle those same flaws? He'll fume under his breath at the driver in the next lane. He'll get the biggest sandwich by showing up early and sidling past the hostess to the buffet line. He'll let six hours of dirty dishes pile up around him and whine that his girlfriend is letting him down.

How would a middle-ground fellow do it? Some of each. Maybe he yells at the other driver, but at the same time he realizes he's overreacting. Maybe he takes the biggest sandwich, but later he shares the leftovers with a dog. And when his girlfriend leaves town, he looks at the pile of dirty dishes and decides he'd better call a housecleaning service. Yet there's no denying he still *has* those fatal flaws of anger, greed and sloth.

He's just a likable guy in spite of it.

That's not to say your protagonist has to follow the middle ground under all circumstances. You could have an incredibly dramatic scene where he fumes under his breath at the driver in the next lane, and the reader will be rooting for him all the way. You could have an equally great scene where he rants about six-going-on-seven weeks of dirty dishes and the reader's heart aches for him.

What makes the difference is how well you set it up – how much we like this guy, in spite of his flaws.

He needs to have flaws, remember? Otherwise he's not interesting; he's got no place to *grow*.

So our job as writers is to create characters who come across as real, plausible people – complete with some bad traits – and who either have what it takes to overcome their flaws so they'll deserve their Happy Ending, or who don't have what it takes so they'll suffer a Tragic Ending.

Whichever they get, the reader will understand it…because they know this character so well.

Picking A Type

Q: I keep going over the descriptions, and I can't decide which type my character is. It's driving me crazy.

A: Then stop reading the descriptions.

Of course an enneagram theorist wouldn't say that. But we're not enneagram theorists, we're writers!

The whole idea is to give ourselves tools that make the job easier, more interesting, more fun. If any of the tools don't *work* for you, there's no point hanging onto 'em.

Any textbook, any style of psychology, any philosophy, is valuable only if it works for you. And if you find yourself going into convoluted back-story to make a character fit some prescription, I'd say throw the prescription overboard. It's not helping.

It's not doing the job it was meant to do.

The only validity to using enneagrams (or astrology, or archetypes, or birth order, or anything else) is if it makes your job easier. But your job is really just to feel like this character works, like this is somebody you could see in real life, reacting in ways that suit your story.

That's it.

Any tool that doesn't make that easier isn't worth keeping.

And of course, any tool that does is a treasure.

I use bits of enneagrams, bits of birth order, bits from chatty interviews, whatever it takes to bring a character to life. We all develop our own sets of tools – probably every writer in the world has a different collection in the toolbox. All that really matters is that the tools in your box work for *you.*

Emotional Baggage

Q: My characters tend to have a lot of emotional baggage, like past hurts and unresolved traumas. Is the fatal flaw a form of emotional baggage?

A: For a great story, baggage is definitely connected to the fatal flaw. If Fred lost his parents in a horrible train wreck when he was ten years old, he could react in a lot of ways…depending on which type he is. In fact, let's do a rundown:

One: he's still angry about the loss, afraid to trust anyone because the parents he trusted were removed without warning.

Two: since he wasn't able to keep his family, he now tries to nurture everyone he meets so at least *somebody* will need/ want him.

Three: if only he'd earned straight A's or made the football team, maybe Mom & Dad would still be here…he'll never deliver a bad performance again.

Four: how can he ever feel complete and happy again when his swell, wonderful, glorious parents were so cruelly taken from him?

Five: here's proof that emotional involvement leads to pain, so it's better to stay detached and use logic rather than emotions.

Six: terrible things can happen at any moment, so he must always be on guard to make sure he and his loved ones stay safe.

Seven: because life is so uncertain and fleeting, the *only* way to live is to make the most of every moment…enjoying the here and now.

Eight: since tragedy can strike anywhere, vigilant leadership is needed to keep innocent people from suffering.

Nine: maybe people feel sorry for him, but hey, he's *fine*… the orphanage served ice cream every Christmas, no problem, everything's *fine*.

You see how, no matter which type Fred is, his response to emotional baggage will fit his type? So exploring his response is a great way of finding his fatal flaw!

Conversely, let's say Fred's co-worker Helen has *no* emotional baggage. She grew up in a happy, loving family with lots of warmth and security and has never suffered anything besides a lost teddy bear at age twelve.

Does that mean she won't have any fatal flaws?

Absolutely not.

Everybody's got 'em. Even all of us wonderfully mentally-healthy writers have them!

Of course we learn, as we grow older and wiser, to temper our flaws. You could work alongside someone for years and never really spot their flaws unless something pretty stressful comes up.

So Helen's fatal flaw might not show up on the surface, but when she's in trouble it sure will. Maybe for her, the trouble is a car accident or a mistaken-identity stalker or something completely unrelated to her virtually non-existent baggage, but she can still experience stress.

And in spite of his dreadful emotional baggage, Fred's fatal flaw might not show up on the surface, either. He might be very skilled at getting around whatever his problem is. Maybe he realized years ago that he's overly cautious, and makes a point – a very careful point – of doing risky things once in a while because he knows it's good for him.

People can and *do* adapt, grow, learn, and change. But when they're under stress, they're more likely to react from whatever their problem area is.

That's one reason so many writer-advice notes say to put your characters in trouble. People in trouble become *more* of what they are. Good or bad. And no matter how good or bad they are, they can always get better or worse...which is lucky for us, because it sets us up for the dramatic ending.

Black Moment

Q: How do fatal flaws contribute to the "all is lost" scene which leads to the depressing or uplifting conclusion?

A: Ideally, the fatal flaw is what leads to the black moment. A truly satisfying black moment doesn't come about because Evil Villain woke up one morning, decided to murder the folks next door, picked up his shotgun and strolled over to John & Mary's plantation.

What makes it better? Say E.V. has chosen to seize John's plantation for taxes – when in fact he could seize *anyone's* plantation, but has always resented John's righteous ranting about the evils of tobacco.

That setup means John's fatal flaw has contributed to his own black moment.

Let's make his contribution even stronger. John is angry about the whole situation, blaming everyone from Evil Villain to the hospital orderlies for this confounded tax notice, and his fury is driving Mary – let's say they've fallen in love – up the wall. If she's going to spend the rest of her life with some man, she wants one who'll calm down and realize that anger doesn't help, who'll quit berating everyone (especially himself), and who'll *forgive* himself for not being able to single-handedly save the world.

So she's packing her bag to return to New England, figuring the hospital will be shut down any minute now, and John is aghast – he's spent his whole life doing the right thing, and now because of it he's going to lose his plantation *and* Mary? That isn't right! He needs to make things right! How can he make things riiiiiiiiight?

Originally John would've stormed through the hospital yelling at the orderlies about how their nursing kept him from clearing enough profit to pay his taxes, but during the course of the book he's started to learn a few things. Seeing Mary packing her bag shows him that getting angry doesn't work, so now he'll have to try something else. He'll have to decide which matters more – the plantation or the woman he loves.

Forgiving Mary for "doing what she believes is right" leads to the awareness that he also needs to forgive himself. And once he's done *that*, his head is clear enough to realize that by converting the entire plantation into hospital grounds, it'll be exempt from taxes… which means Evil Villain can't foreclose.

So now John is heading over to the county courthouse to sign the hospital-conversion papers, and Mary sees him from the stagecoach window. Stunned that he's willing to make such a sacrifice for the good of her patients, she races after him and says he *must* keep the plantation, even if it means switching half of the hospital rooms to tobacco fields, and she'll be proud to live there with him (and Junior) happily ever after.

Could be a happy ending, right there.

Or at that point, John might realize that it wasn't so much the plantation he wanted as it was a feeling of security, which he gets from Mary's love even more than he got it from acres of tobacco. So he'll suggest they take the stagecoach to New England, help Louisa May Alcott roll bandages, and live happily ever after.

But you see how his fatal flaw is responsible for the black moment? And how, once he overcomes it, he deserves that happy ending?

That outcome is what your readers have been rooting for all along – and the more John is responsible for his own black moment *and* his own triumph, the happier they'll be.

Changing Types

Q: Can characters change their personality type after some traumatic experience? For instance, might a Five nerd become a Seven adventurer as the result of a near-death experience?

A: The deal is, we are what we are. But even so, there's a lot of room for change within each of the nine types.

Taking the example of a nerdy Five (it's okay for me to call 'em nerds because I *am* a Five) who decides to become adventurous like a Seven – that can happen, absolutely.

Say I decide I'm gonna throw caution to the winds and fly to Las Vegas on the spur of the moment and bet half my income on 32 red. The idea is giving me chills of horror, just *typing* it, but we'll say I'm behaving out of character after this near-death experience.

So maybe on the plane I'll calculate the odds of the roulette wheel coming up 32 red and decide to bet on something with stronger odds. (Although I'm getting out of my league, here; we need somebody who knows roulette!) Even so, I'm still living more adventurously. I place the bet, win or lose, and maybe order sushi because I've never eaten that before, and decide to hit the stage for karaoke.

But my character hasn't changed. Even while I'm up there singing "I Will Survive" – or whatever is the most extreme karaoke song imaginable – I'm still observing. "Hmm, that guy in the third row looks interested. Wonder what he's doing after the show?" Still studying. "The sushi comes with a lot more rice than I like; maybe next time I should order a side of ahi tuna." Still analyzing. "If I'd flown Southwest instead of American I might've gotten better mileage points." You see how that works?

It definitely *is* possible to change the outward factors of life. Look at teenagers, who try on a new personality every few weeks! But the inner self doesn't truly change.

And it doesn't need to. Because every type can be absolutely wonderful, can be absolutely fulfilled, just by taking a few steps toward health and balance and all those other great things which lead to the triumphant conclusion of your book.

Resolution Timing

Q: Should each of my main characters resolve their flaws at the same time?

A: I've seen wonderful books where the main characters overcome their flaws at the same instant, and where they do it a few scenes (or a few hundred miles) apart, and both ways work fine.

It's a matter of whatever will give you the best drama for that particular story.

Look at the books you've enjoyed most. (Not saying you have to write that particular type of book, but they're sure more fun to analyze than books you *didn't* especially enjoy.) I bet you can pinpoint the moment where each of the main characters overcomes their fatal flaw.

Maybe it was halfway through, and they spent the rest of the book waiting for someone else to catch up while you rooted for them all the way. Maybe it was in the last paragraph, and left you hugely relieved that they finally made it. Maybe it was at the exact same moment as everyone else onstage, and left you crying for joy.

There's sure no One Best Moment to make characters overcome their fatal flaws.

It's a matter of what works for the story.

And what works for your story might not work for mine. That's good. That's what makes different readers love different authors, and why each of us writers has a chance to reach people who think we're the Greatest Novelist Ever while they wouldn't waste their time on our best critique buddy. (Forget about those people who'd rather read our critique buddy; they're just not Our Readers.)

I'm getting off on a soapbox tangent, here, but there are so *many* different readers looking for writers they'll love. Millions of 'em love Dan Brown and Nora Roberts, sure. But I bet all of us have writers we love who aren't worldwide bestsellers. Yet when we see them come out with a new title, we're thrilled, we can't wait to read it.... Those are our Own Special Writers.

And each one was discovered by an editor who spotted the same thing we did.

I like what author Jennifer Crusie says: the important thing is to find an editor who loves your work. An editor who recognizes that, while you might not be the entire world's favorite writer, there's something that a certain number of readers will love about you. It doesn't matter if no other editor sees that; all you need is the one who believes in you.

Isn't that a wonderful thing to contemplate?

Somewhere out there in the world are the readers just waiting for what you can give them. When they find you, you're going to be their Own Special Writer.

It's such a tremendous privilege, and when you hear from a reader who *gets* what you do, there's no greater feeling in the world.

Impossible Combos

Q: According to the charts, my character can't actually be what I think she is, a Two and a Seven. Should I give her the quiz from your website "workshops" again, or might she just be schizo?

A: Schizo. Definitely.

No, no, no! Just joking. (And, boy, I wish I could insert a smile symbol here.)

It's possible, of course, that she'll come out different if you repeat the quiz. And if you'd like to try a longer version, you can find several (including some for free) online at www.Enneagram Institute.com.

But that's not the only possibility.

Maybe she *does* have traits of both Two and Seven, even though the charts say that can't happen. Unless you're a diehard enneagram purist, though, of course it can happen!

It could be this character is out partying till dawn every night, and on the way home she's counseling the cab driver: "You know, if you roll your shoulders you won't feel nearly so tense at the end of a nine-mile drive."

Absolutely plausible. No problem with such a combination, even if (in theory) it can't happen.

Look at us. We're *all* bundles of contradictions. Remember that example about how you might be a Democrat but love Ronald Reagan, or an agnostic but enjoy Midnight Mass, or live in the city but wear country clothes, or love dogs but hate the neighbor's dog?

Nothing says we're always going to make sense, on the surface.

Nothing says your character has to, either.

If she's telling the cab driver how to relax his shoulders, maybe even offering him an aspirin from her Gucci bag which she adores because she picked it up at the most fabulous sale with her friend what's-his-name two weeks ago…sure, it might seem a little bit contradictory on the surface.

But does it sound plausible? Yep.

We see that she has a truly caring heart. She can be pursuing adventure all over the place, but *still* nurturing the people around her.

What matters is plausibility. And as long as your character has that, who cares what the chart says?

Matter of fact, when I stagger down from the karaoke stage, I hope she's right there with an aspirin from her Gucci bag!

Revealing Flaws

Q: How do I strike a balance? I want to reveal my character's fatal flaw, but I don't want to hit the reader over the head with it.

A: Hitting over the head is a great image. Because we've all seen this done badly, right?

And we've all seen it done well – although we haven't likely stopped to admire it during the middle of the read, because the story is just too interesting.

So what makes the difference? It's like any other tool of character. Appearance, for instance.

Eight consecutive paragraphs about the color of the heroine's eyes is a bit (okay, maybe more than a bit) over the top. So is eight consecutive paragraphs about the heroine's fatal flaw.

But the fatal flaw is part of her personality, right? It affects her outlook on life, it affects her behavior, it affects her choice of career and dress and friends. It affects how she thinks, how she feels, what she does.

And we'll see that.

Say Mary has always yearned to be needed. She brought home stray kittens, she tucked her dolls into bed every night, she'd sit up listening to Grandpa's corny jokes until midnight every night because he seemed lonely.

So we really don't need to read, "Mary has always yearned to be needed." Because we'll *see* her walking to work at the hospital, worried about getting there on time, but stopping to help Mrs. Dexter across the street. By itself, that scene is a hit-over-the-head: "Look, see, she's helping an old lady across the street! What does that show you, huh? Huh?"

But let's say that during this scene, Mrs. Dexter reveals that John is about to plow the north forty and Mary realizes she's got to stop him. Now there's a purpose to the scene besides just showing her desire to nurture. She gets Mrs. D to the curb and Mrs. D says "you've always been such a sweetheart" and Mary says "oh, you know I always love chatting with you" before scurrying off, but we've seen a plot point that advances the story.

We may not know yet whether Mary helped the old lady in hopes of getting info on John, or because she's a naturally helpful person.

But a few hours later, the neighbor who gives her a ride back from the hospital will report that "those kittens you brought Susan are doing fine" and she'll think "whew, glad that worked."

Then she'll be ready to head home from work but still feel like something's left undone, and look around to see if anyone else needs anything before she locks the door.

It's all setting up her compulsion to be needed. We don't yet need to know *why* she feels this way; we can learn that later on. We're just seeing who she is, what she does, and that's enough to set up her fatal flaw.

The flaw hasn't even gotten her in trouble yet, unless helping Mrs. D across the street made her late for work…but before long it will, because we've written that into the plot. We're putting this dogged nurturer up against the dogged perfectionist, and there's going to be trouble.

But the revelation that Mary Yearns To Be Needed doesn't have to happen all at once. In fact, it shouldn't – that's beating the reader over the head. Trickling in the information, though, is tremendously effective. Charles Dickens said, "Make them laugh. Make them cry. Make them wait."

So that's where the balance comes in: delivering the information a little bit at a time, and always in context of what's happening at the moment. It's a handy technique, and the readers will never notice what you've done – all they'll notice is how real your character seems.

Designing A Character

Q: Whenever I build a character I take a few traits from a neighbor, another few from a friend, an appearance from someone at work, an attitude from someone else, and so on. Is that totally off base?

A: I think any tool that *works* for you can never be off base!

If it doesn't feel like this one's working, though, it might be because it's edging close to what author Cheryl Reavis calls "the Mr. Potato Head approach" to creating characters.

For anybody who didn't grow up playing Mr. Potato Head, the idea was that this game contained a plastic potato with little holes into which you could insert your choice of various wacky-looking eyes, noses, mouths, arms and legs.

I don't remember what the object of the game was…maybe simply to make the wackiest potato. But it's possible that taking various character traits at random and then using them to form a character from scratch might result in a Mr. Potato Head type of person – just kind of a hodgepodge.

Now, of course we're all a hodgepodge in real life. But for fiction, we flat-out don't have *room* for too many contradictory traits. To keep the story moving swiftly enough to fit it within the book covers, we've gotta pare down the character traits to just the essentials that matter, and let the rest go.

The Mr. Potato Head approach might work just beautifully and wind up giving you a person who feels integrated, natural, whole. But if it doesn't, you might want to try starting with just the most essential trait about the character…the thing which (at least for purposes of this book) defines who they are.

Then shape the other characteristics around that. Say, Rob is a man who's never had a family because he was raised by wolves in the forest and, during the part of his life that's covered in this story, he wants to know what it's like to love and be loved.

Of course that wouldn't be his mission at the beginning of the book; at the beginning it would be to stop the wolf trappers or whatever. It's only as the book unfolds that we readers – and eventually Rob – will discover his core motivation.

But for now, say that wanting a family is Rob's essential trait for purposes of this book. What does that tell us about him as a person?

What kind of characteristics would such a person have?

What kind of decisions would he have made about his life up to this point?

How are they working out for him?

What, if anything, does he want to change about his life? What would he resist changing?

How does he handle threats?

What makes him happy? What makes him wistful?

What does he do about it?

Probably everyone reading this would answer slightly differently, depending on their vision of Rob. Which is great – there's no way we're all going to write the exact same book even when handed a character with the same core motivation.

But you see how answering questions like those might make Rob seem a little more integrated than assigning him random traits? Worth a try, if you ever decide the random-traits system isn't working.

If it *is*, though, by all means stick with it – because every writer has a unique set of tools, and there's no point changing something that works!

Wrapping Up

Enneagrams and fatal flaws are wonderful tools. They aren't a prescription, though. Every writer will use them differently, which is what makes writing so rewarding.

We all put our own spin on every character, every scene, every story we create. And the easiest way to prove that is to imagine that everyone who reads this book came across an assignment saying, "Write a story about a Type Eight who goes to Five with an Intimacy subtype and a Two wing," and did it.

You can tell what would happen, right?

No two stories would be the same.

We writers have so much creativity inside us, so many ways of bringing new people to life, that we don't *need* prescriptions for what to write.

All we really need is a pencil and, once in a while, a few other helpful tools.

That's where enneagrams come in.

I hope you enjoy them!

APPENDIX: Wings & Connections

This section is for people who just can't get enough of enneagram theory!

As discussed on page 7, each type shows some characteristics of the types on either side (its wings) and *also* goes to two other types (its connections).

Some theorists say that people "go to" one type when they're stressed, and another when they're healthy, but others say both types can be good or bad. And as writers, we can use whatever theory will give us the most compelling characters.

Your characters might go to both of their connections, neither of them, or only one – and the same is true of their wings.

Here's how they line up:

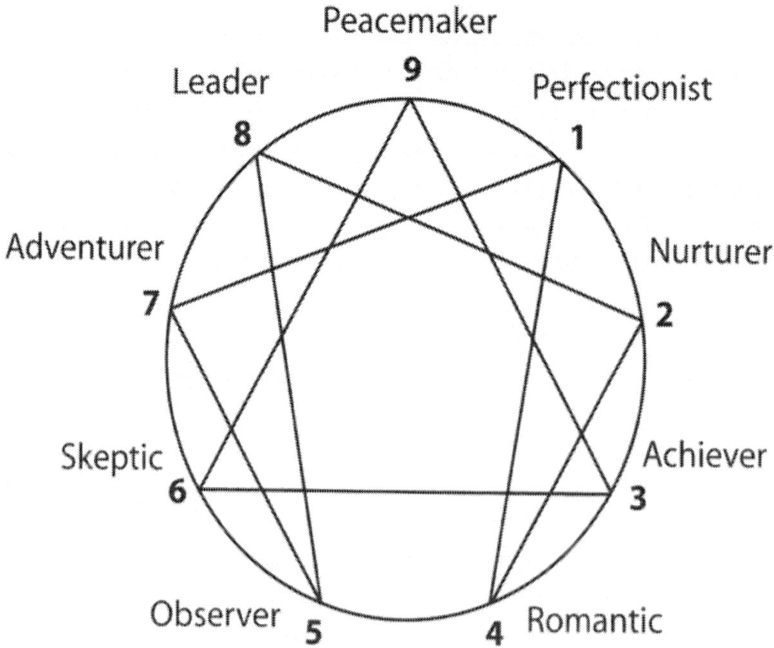

TYPE ONE

Ones With A Two Wing

Ones with a Two wing have a natural place to direct their idealistic hopes of making the world a better place. Improving things for other people is a mission they'll adopt with enthusiasm, because it lets them combine their passion for perfection with a genuine concern about the well-being of people they care for.

Relationships matter deeply to these Ones. On the positive side, they're wonderfully helpful, empathetic and sensitive to other people. On the negative side, they're more image-conscious and controlling...because they want other people to see the best in them.

But where most Ones tend to be somewhat rigid in their judgments, those with a Two wing are less so. They'll put individual needs ahead of their global ideals, and they'll devote their passion for perfection to causes which help others. Teaching, nursing, whatever will make life better for people – whether or not these are people they know personally. They don't save their caring attention solely for their own circle of friends and family.

While a typical One might be more involved with the quest for perfection on a worldwide scale, the Two-wing Ones concentrate more on individuals. Theory is less important than actual people, and even if they can't help lecturing those people on the right way to live, it's always with a greater degree of personal warmth.

Ones With A Nine Wing

Ones are fascinated with principles of right and wrong, good and bad, and those with a Nine wing apply their theories on a scale that's less personal and more functional. They're not particularly bothered if the family next door uses dangerous pesticides on the rose garden, but they'll write well-reasoned letters to the pesticide manufacturer.

These Ones are so rational and fair-minded that they might seem to be uninvolved with everyday human contact. They're more devoted to abstract principles than to specific individuals, and are likely to find more satisfaction in the spiritual beauty of nature or art than in the waitress at the corner deli.

Because individual concerns don't get in their way, Nine-wing Ones make the best judges and advocates. They can argue brilliantly when it comes to ethical questions, and they tend to be more objective about any issues that strike close to home. Some people might even accuse them of being colorless, because they pay more attention to principles than to their own appearance...or their own relationships.

What matters to them is the big picture, and they're skilled at maintaining objectivity. If that means coming across as impersonal, so be it. Pleasing any individual doesn't matter nearly as much as upholding global standards of justice and truth.

Ones Going To Four

Because feelings are the most important thing to Fours, Ones who go in that direction will be more inclined than most to pay attention to their feelings.

Even so, they have to work at uncovering their actual feelings, rather than simply those which reflect the most correct outlook and behavior. But this is a great opportunity for Ones to become more aware of what they actually feel, not just what they ought to feel.

With Four's tendency to regret the unattainable, it's easy to see the One growing morose over how far the world falls short of expectations. It's also easy to see the One growing morose over personal flaws – "I'm a failure; I took an extra cookie and I didn't wave at the neighbor and I forgot to floss last night."

Too much of that, and this One might give up all hope of achieving perfection and instead dive into a binge cycle. "I'm such a horrible slob, I might as well have *three* extra cookies. No, five. No, twelve!"

But if a One going to Four runs the risk of turning that fatal-flaw anger inward and getting depressed, there's also a likelihood of benefiting from the Four's gift for creativity.

A One who picks up on the Four passion for self-expression through art will have a wonderful new venue for sharing deeply held beliefs about the world, about good and evil, and about whatever themes cry out to be shared.

Ones Going To Seven

For someone who spends each moment of the day trying to live up to the highest possible standards of right and good, there's tremendous appeal in the notion of simply letting go and enjoying whatever spontaneous pleasures life has to offer.

Ones who go to Seven get to do this. A classic example might be a One who devotes every waking minute to the job, but who goes on vacation and becomes a whole new person. Playful, cheerful, flexible, sensual…open to whatever might happen next.

It's quite a contradiction from One's usual self. And if a One doesn't go to Seven often, the trip can be startling. After an entire year of squelching every desire for freedom, suddenly abandoning all the conventional wisdom of morality and restraint might lead to – well, let's call it excess.

Which might lead to guilt or anxiety. Which would put the One right back into the usual constraints of Always Doing What's Correct.

But Ones who accept the Seven side of their nature and make a point of relaxing and acknowledging their own desires every once in a while – certainly more often than once a year – will benefit from letting some new freedom into their world. They'll be more natural, enthusiastic and optimistic people…not only while on vacation, but also in everyday life.

TYPE TWO

Twos With A One Wing

When Twos take on the One wing, they place more emphasis on ethics. They still work to make life better for others, but now their mission is more on a global scale rather than simply in their own back yard. These are the people most likely to work for a good, philanthropic cause, and the people most likely to operate a charity or establish a foundation.

They'll have more respect for the boundaries of others, so they're less likely to invade in the name of assistance. But they can still be domineering, explaining that such control is justified because "it's for Sarah's own good."

Ones rarely allow themselves to want anything they view as wrong or lazy or less than ideal, and Twos are already skilled at ignoring their own desires. So this combination makes them even more likely to devote all their attention to serving others, as well as to feel guilty about their own unexpressed needs.

The best way to avoid feeling guilty is to follow all the rules, all the time, and the One-wing Twos will set up strong rules about looking out for the good of the world and the good of their loved ones. They'll beat up on themselves if they ever fail to love with all their hearts, because they judge themselves by the highest possible standards. Still, their solid rules are balanced by emotional warmth, making them wonderful teachers.

Twos With A Three Wing

Three's sense of glamour enhances the Two's natural sociability, and these people are extremely good at getting things done. When it comes to a project that serves the well-being of others, you couldn't ask for a better, more efficient worker than a Three-wing Two.

Since Threes care about looking good in front of the world, these Twos will have an extra dimension of vanity. It might show up as self-importance – "look at how essential I am, look at how everyone depends on me" – but these people are so charming and outgoing that nobody minds their grand positioning.

They're extremely good at getting their way, combining the Two's ability to discern what people want with the Three's ability to cultivate beneficial relationships. While some might call them manipulative, ambitious or calculating types who use people to validate their own desirability, others will see them as genuinely warm, personable Twos who enjoy being around friends.

Either way, they'll be wonderfully self-assured. They make great communicators, able to reach many people on a high level of warmth, and they thrive on the pressure of accomplishing several projects at once. If you want someone to bring together a group of people, inspire them and send them home feeling like friends, here's exactly the person you need.

Twos Going To Four

Twos have a hard time identifying their own needs, and going to Four makes that job much easier. They're better able to develop and maintain an inner life, focusing on their own emotional complexity as well as the needs of everyone around them.

Because Fours are all about creativity, drama and big emotions, these Twos will display those same traits. That can be wonderful if they uncover some artistic self-expression and learn to express their feelings rather than denying any individual needs. That can be awful if they become obsessive about their loved ones, giving way to mournful self-pity and depression over how much they've done for others and how little they've done for themselves.

Either way, though, they're more likely to get in touch with their own feelings, both the joyful ones and the anguished ones. The Four gift for emotional honesty makes these Twos better able to understand themselves as easily as they understand others, and gives them the ability to address their own needs along with those of everyone else.

Honoring their own individuality lets them maintain a more solid sense of self, finding other ways to feel worthwhile besides simply helping whoever's nearby. They might still fear being alone, with all the Four angst over the pain of abandonment, but they have more confidence in their ability to cope with life on their own.

Twos Going To Eight

Eight's gift for self-assertion can come in handy for these Twos, who otherwise might never speak up about what they want for themselves.

On the other hand, it can also make them more aggressive when it comes to helping whomever they've chosen as the recipient of their attention – not necessarily a stalker mentality, but a determination that Jim is going to eat this good healthy chicken soup no matter *what* it takes to make him open his mouth and swallow.

The Twos who go to Eight are better able to get things done, because they're more self-confident and straightforward rather than worried about the good opinion of others. This makes them very effective at communicating, simply putting out what they want to say instead of working for the most acceptable way to say it.

Even if they might be considered overly blunt, they're good at leadership. They're not afraid to be honest, and they're not afraid of taking charge. When someone asks for more than they're willing to give, they have no problem refusing.

It's easy for an Eight to set boundaries, and Twos need that skill. Of course, they can go overboard and become downright hard or cruel if they take it to extremes. Yet a good balance of selfishness and service to others can make them not only healthier, but better able to care for everyone around them...including themselves.

TYPE THREE

Threes With A Two Wing

Threes who lean more toward the Two side of their personality are even more involved with those around them than other Threes might be. Their leadership skills are as strong as you'd expect from any Three, but are enhanced by a genuine desire to help people.

Of course, all Threes care about social approval, but those with a Two wing care even more deeply. They value the opinion of others not only because looking good matters, but because personal relationships matter as well.

Even if there aren't many personal relationships in this Three's life, the few that exist will be vital. Because the relationship matters so much, the Three won't settle for just admiration and approval. While attention and approval are highly desirable goals, love is even more desirable.

So in order to ensure that the love keeps coming, Threes with a Two wing become even more skilled at sensing the wants and needs of those around them...and delivering whatever will get the desired results.

These Threes go well beyond the usual – already high – standards for their type. They're *more* affectionate, more helpful and more generous. On the other hand, they can be *more* possessive, more jealous and more boastful.

Either way, they bring to their relationships all the warmth and caring, all the sparkling enthusiasm and dedicated effort, that anyone could possibly want.

Threes With A Four Wing

Threes who show more Four characteristics display a more artistic, sensitive and dramatic side than ordinary Threes. They keep to themselves a little more, analyzing their feelings in greater detail. Some people might think they're haughty or aloof, but in fact they're simply more focused on the constant ebb and flow of creative, emotional moods that constitute their everyday life.

Since Fours like things to be larger-than-life, and Threes are gifted at shining their light for the world to see, the two together can be remarkably grand. And since Fours are more aware of feelings and emotions than a typical Three, those Threes with a Four wing have a more strongly developed sense of intuition and imagination. They can see deeper, interpret better, and use their insights for any purpose they choose.

The healthy Threes use their insights for humanistic purposes, while those who haven't yet actualized their best self might lean more toward melodrama or moodiness. Either way, they can be tremendously successful as artists, as creators, and as teachers with a unique flair for reaching others.

While all Fours tend to be creative, Threes with a Four wing might use that creativity in a variety of areas. The arts are a possibility, but so are business, education and science. Regardless of where they apply their skills, these Four-wing Threes are certain to excel.

Threes Going To Six

Because Sixes are devoted to loyalty and commitment, Threes who go in that direction display more of each trait than might otherwise be found in a Three.

Whether their loyalty is to a person or a cause, a job or a region, a belief or a relationship, they'll back it with wholehearted passion. This gives them outstanding moral courage, as well as the ability to maintain an ethical stance which might be tough for others to uphold. With their shining gift for leadership, these Threes can inspire others to uphold a commitment to their most treasured cause.

Going to Six can make it harder, though, for Threes to give up their constant pursuit of success. The Six's tendency toward identifying with the existing power structure, hierarchy and tradition means these Threes are even less likely to acknowledge any possible flaws of their own.

And because Six's fatal flaw is fear, the Three who's already hiding any vulnerabilities behind a mask of constant perfection will have plenty of opportunities to be afraid. It's easy to become hyperactive, knowing that any slip just might mean the dreaded prospect of (gasp) failure.

However, those who *do* face their fears of failure are likely to discover that authentic feelings *can* be expressed, and it doesn't mean the end of the world. The realization that they can admit some vulnerability and still survive is a wonderful reward for Threes who've spent a lifetime working to live up to expectations.

Threes Going To Nine

If Threes are constantly driven, while Nines are steadily tranquil, you can imagine the contrasts of a Three who goes to Nine. These people who normally spend every minute seeking out new opportunities for achievement will appreciate the value of taking time to relax, of slowing down, of spending an idle afternoon with friends and simply savoring the leisure.

At their best, Threes who go to Nine will realize that success is more a matter of perspective than a certain salary or title or ranking. They can simply be who they are, following the interests that truly appeal to them, rather than performing a role which they hope will earn enough acclaim to let them feel loved.

At their worst, these Threes will take on the Nine's flaw of sloth, or emotional numbness. They may decide that since they can't become the best in their field within six weeks, they might as well give up and retreat to apathy. It's unusual, though, to see a Three become passive to the point of depression.

Instead, they're more likely to pursue Nine's gift for tranquility by scheduling time for relaxation, by allowing themselves to take in more of the world around them – without having to live up to constantly escalating standards of performance – and by seeking out projects which carry personal meaning rather than those which carry the promise of public recognition.

By applying their skills to projects that genuinely interest them, these Threes serve not only themselves but everyone who benefits from their always brilliant work.

TYPE FOUR

Fours With A Three Wing

Since Fours have a creative flair to begin with, and Threes know how to make the best impression at all times, you can imagine how sociable, extroverted and even flamboyant this person will be. Very upbeat, energetic and productive. Very active, outgoing and image-conscious. A Four with a Three wing will always be aware of the need to impress other people, and will almost always do a fabulous job of it.

Fours yearn for attention and special treatment, and Threes know just how to achieve it. They're ambitious, even competitive, and aren't afraid of going for the most elite or most prestigious slot they can find.

For that matter, they won't hesitate to go after the most attractive person in the room, because they're good at envisioning their "ideal mate" on whomever looks right for the part. They carry out their part by dressing well, making a distinctive impression, and are known for strong social skills as well as strong organizational skills.

There may be a division, though, between these Fours' public lives and private lives. They might be the toast of the office, but then go home to a lonely apartment (an apartment that's beautifully decorated). They may have a gloriously happy home life, but never mention it while concentrating on work. While Fours are always aware of strong feelings, they may choose to hide those feelings if their Three side perceives any social disadvantage to sharing their emotions.

Fours With A Five Wing

Fours lead with their heart, and Fives lead with their head. So when a Four who feels overwhelmed by emotion goes into an analytical or intellectual mode, the result is an original, unconventional thinker...someone with an incredible depth of insight.

These people will have a spiritual as well as an aesthetic openness, an ability to see multiple levels of meaning in virtually everything. They may seem enigmatic or distant, immersed in a world of complex creativity, but they're always very much their own person.

Of course, it's easy to see how they might feel set apart from the rest of the world. Four's sense of "not really belonging" is intensified by Five's tendency toward withdrawal. Other people may describe them as serious or reserved or hard to read, possibly even alienated or reclusive.

But when this Four opens up, it's like an instant sunrise. Whatever was held back is suddenly in full view, ready for the world to marvel at. Or for the world to ignore.

Fours with a Five wing need to pour themselves into their work, their art, but they don't need public recognition for it. What matters is the expression of their own unique views, their own distinctive way of looking at the world, whether through science or philosophy or art. Their blend of emotional and intellectual strength almost always creates something remarkable.

Fours Going To One

Fours who take on some One characteristics are, just as you'd expect, practical and well-organized and ready to act on their ideals. They have a gift for objectivity, which makes them less likely to be controlled by their feelings and more likely to work toward realistic goals.

Naturally, Fours and Ones both have their own vision of what a perfect world should be. So when you get a Four who goes to One, that vision is going to be incredibly strong.

On the negative side, it may lead the Four so far down the road of perfectionistic fault-finding that any hope of creativity is stifled. Instead, grandiose ideas are presented as absolute truth.

But on the positive side, a Four with the dogged practicality of a One will be more of a contributor than a complainer. More of a doer than a dreamer. More in touch with reality, and able to minimize a tendency toward melodrama in favor of actual problem-solving.

One's habit of discipline is a good balance for Four's habit of self-indulgence, although if that discipline is carried to extremes the Four might become overly self-critical, nit-picky or guilt-ridden.

However, Fours with the One ability to put aside their own feelings strike a wonderful balance between idealism and action... expecting the best of everyone, including themselves, and doing whatever it takes to deliver that.

Fours Going To Two

Put an emotionally open Four with a nurturing Two, and you've got a model of empathetic warmth. Going to Two makes a Four, who's already good at understanding the feelings of others, even *more* caring and accepting.

It's hard to imagine a better combination for the kind of teacher or therapist or minister you'll look back on with gratitude for years after basking in their warm acceptance.

These Fours are more accommodating than average, and less self-absorbed. It's always possible they might be fleeing their own emotions by focusing on those of others, but it's just as likely that they're embracing the ideal of service to others. Either way, their interpersonal skills are extremely strong.

They're good at identifying with whomever they talk to, and can offer a better listening ear than virtually any other type. This easy identification, if taken to extremes, can result in codependency or manipulation – becoming fixated on a loved one and taking compulsive pride in being needed.

But a better result is a Four who bonds well, who cheerfully accommodates others, and who shares private perceptions of what's beautiful in life with anyone lucky enough to be nearby.

Warmth and passion, understanding and acceptance...what more could anyone want?

TYPE FIVE

Fives With A Four Wing

Fives who lean more toward the Four side of their personality offer a wonderful combination of rational insight and emotional sensitivity. They have enough romance in their souls to see the beauty in a math formula, or the beauty in truth.

Combining the typical Five intellect with the artistic vision of a Four helps them reflect the best union of knowledge and intuition, of fact and fancy. They're more creative than ordinary Fives, and they're also more humanistic.

On the down side, they might wind up displaying too much of the Four's characteristic envy, viewing others from a superior intellectual distance while envying their ability to form easy emotional connections. Those big, sweeping feelings of regret might overcome them whenever they see themselves as too self-absorbed.

A Five with the typical Four gift for reading others' emotions can be a gifted counselor or analyst, although they might also use analysis as a way of keeping people at a safe distance.

Fives tend to be reclusive no matter what, and the dramatic Four wing can push them toward grand isolation as a shield for any emotional vulnerability. But those who trust their feelings can be wonderfully sensitive and empathetic. When they honor both their emotional insight and their gift for clear-headed observation, they're a tremendous asset to any relationship.

Fives With A Six Wing

Fives who show more Six characteristics are extremely loyal, with a deep capacity for friendship and commitment. They're not only committed to family and friends, but also to their beliefs, whatever those might be.

However, they have difficulty trusting people at first. It can be tough for them to identify their own feelings, which makes sharing feelings with others – or even with themselves – a major challenge.

But regardless of their emotions, they're firmly committed to getting the job done. These Fives are hard workers, who care more about doing their duty than about personal comfort. You can imagine how this puts them in great demand for long-term, difficult assignments.

As with all Sixes, they tend to be cautious about things. Anxiety is nothing new to them, and neither is skepticism. When it comes to academic work, though, particularly in the physical and social sciences, that skepticism comes in handy.

It also accompanies the typical Five detachment, which results in a good sense of humor. More than other Fives, those with a Six wing are known for intellectual playfulness – they're very comfortable examining every facet of a problem and coming up with solutions no one else would ever notice.

Fives Going To Seven

While all Fives are thinkers, those who go to Seven are also doers.

They still value knowledge, of course, but they value experience as well. So instead of spending every free minute in their ivory tower, they'll come outside and toss a ball around before coming up with a list of words that rhyme with "spherical" or a new method for measuring speed. Although they never stop thinking about things, they'll let themselves do things while they think.

When all goes well, these Fives enjoy a far broader experience of life than those who don't go to Seven. When things go badly, though, they might take on too many projects at once. Their passion for knowledge can lead them down any number of avenues, but too many avenues can make even the most dedicated observer somewhat scattered and distracted.

Impulsiveness can be wonderful for Fives who need a break from non-stop thinking, and the best Seven traits make them more fun-loving and less inhibited.

A typical Five might be self-conscious in a social setting, or any setting where there's no specific intellectual goal, but one who embodies Seven characteristics will be more likely to go with the flow and enjoy whatever's happening in the present moment.

Fives Going To Eight

Fives who go to Eight appreciate the importance of mastery – not only of their own mind, but also of the world around them. They're more concerned with hands-on deeds, not just with thoughts.

While the typical Five might be detached from the world except on an intellectual level, this one will be more engaged. The realization that "I don't have to know everything about a situation before taking action" can be wonderfully liberating, and a Five who realizes that will be more ready to meet the world head on.

Trying things out in real life is a great confidence-builder, and repeated success makes it easier for these Eight-wing Fives to trust their instincts. This will make them more spontaneous, more free to take action without thinking through every detail, certain that they can handle whatever comes up.

Staying detached means setting aside any strong emotions, but these Fives don't hesitate to acknowledge their feelings. Instead of withdrawing from a nosy boss or a heckling neighbor, they're able to set clear limits of what they'll tolerate and what they won't.

Fives who go to Eight find it easier to stay in touch with their physical self, so they can call on the body as well as the brain to meet any situation that arises.

TYPE SIX

Sixes With A Five Wing

Sixes who show some Five traits tend to be intellectual, studious and reclusive. No surprise there, right? Combining a "life of the mind" orientation with a "can't be too careful" outlook is bound to produce somebody who's good at predicting the future, thanks to extremely careful analysis of the past.

Since both types can be highly original, a Five-winged Six is likely to impress you with perspectives nobody else has ever spotted. Some people might call them downright idiosyncratic, and that's certainly a possibility. In any case, they're likely to come up with an original take on things, and wonder why everyone around them is so surprised by what seems obvious.

On the positive side, this Six will likely be skillful, serious and soft-spoken. On the negative side, there's a possibility of intellectual arrogance, cynicism or even paranoia. Anyone who doesn't trust easily, and who's capable of in-depth research on why trust might be a mistake, will be great at coming up with legal solutions and crafty angles…but not so great at winning friends.

However, once this person is your friend, you definitely have a friend for life. Such a Six has extremely keen insight into what makes you (and the entire world) tick, and winning the approval of this shrewd observer is the kind of triumph you can treasure for a lifetime.

Sixes With A Seven Wing

The Seven's playful spontaneity is a stark contrast to the Six's determined caution, so this wing will provide some expansion. Six is always good with friends, but the Seven wing adds an even more sociable dimension. This person makes no secret of wanting to be liked, of valuing companionship, and can be disarmingly funny when it comes to winning a friend.

With such energy always on board, they can become over-active to the point of frenzy, taking carefree impulsivity a little too far. They might feel threatened by minor things, lashing out with unfounded accusations or seeming impossible to please. Another dimension would be irritability or even extreme anxiety, to the point of debilitating panic attacks.

However, the Six's usual caution can help rein in the more manic side of Seven, meaning the best of both worlds shows up in someone who'd be described as lively or ingratiating or extroverted. Someone you want at your next party!

Sixes often develop humor as a resource, and the Seven wing makes them even more likely to use it. They might not be looking for a close relationship, but they'll deflect any attempts at closeness with such entertaining wit that nobody can take offense. Again, what better person to enjoy at a party?

Sixes Going To Three

Sixes and Threes are both known for working hard, and this person won't hesitate to play hard as well. The best way to avoid anxiety is by keeping busy, and becoming a workaholic is a pretty sure way to stay busy. But hobbies work just as well, as do sports and arts and any other pursuit the Six chooses.

How to choose? With Three's usual concern for the right image. Taking on the optimal role or image will help the Six feel more secure, better able to impress others, better able to guarantee security in life. If that means occasionally lying, well, it's for a good cause. Besides, what matters most is doing an outstanding job – no matter what it takes.

While these Sixes may occasionally be reluctant to try something new because of the risk of failure, they're usually more willing to take action than Sixes who don't go to Three. By and large, they feel good about everything they accomplish, and take pride in excellent performance no matter what the venue.

Solid performance means feeling secure, so this Six tends to be pretty self-confident and optimistic. Sure, things can always go wrong, but Three's skill at staying productive and maintaining a successful image will provide reassurance whenever it's needed.

Sixes Going To Nine

Because Nines tend to be calm and accepting most of the time, Sixes who go in that direction will be more inclined to trust other people rather than suspecting hidden motives. They're less likely to take life too seriously, and more likely to trust their own inner authority than to seek confirmation from outside themselves.

Of course, if they take this laid-back attitude too far, they might wind up stuck in apathy, falling into comfortable habits with no thought of anything else, numbing themselves with work or food or sleep or whatever will quiet any voice of anxiety within. But the Nine's ability to see every possible side of a question helps the Six look at the world through a bigger lens, and that helps them become more aware of – and respectful of – their own feelings.

Their gift for seeing the big picture tends to make them more stable and self-possessed, more open to new ideas, and also more receptive to others' viewpoints.

This broader perspective makes them good at offering support to those who need it, because they recognize what it's like to want support and reassurance. Sixes who go to Nine are able to turn that need around and help others in the same situation, empathizing as no other type can.

TYPE SEVEN

Sevens With A Six Wing

Sevens who take on the characteristics of Sixes are more sensitive types. They'll place more emphasis on commitment and responsibility than most Sevens, and they won't spend nearly as much time resisting any sense of constriction. Rules won't bother them quite as much.

Instead of going for short-term enjoyment, the Six-wing Sevens are willing to put more time into building and maintaining relationships.

They're also more willing to experience anxiety rather than fleeing it through the pursuit of adventure. In fact, they might seem downright insecure at times, more hesitant than a typical Seven and more vulnerable to the possibility of hurt. But because they're willing to admit when they feel insecure or afraid, these Sevens are more in tune with their own feelings and less likely to stay constantly on the move.

Their facility with language is enhanced by the Six's gift for wit, and they can be wonderfully playful. Instead of viewing life as a quest for more of everything, they can appreciate the value of contrasts. Spontaneity is balanced by dependability, resilience is balanced by caution, and high spirits are balanced by good sense.

Sevens have such great people skills already that they magnify the Six tendency to be ingratiating. Potential friends will feel very special indeed, faced with a combination of quiet intimacy and gregarious charm.

Sevens With An Eight Wing

An Eight wing makes the already outgoing, exuberant Seven even more so. The feeling that "the world is mine for the taking" becomes stronger, because while Seven enjoys sampling various experiences and moving on, Eight won't hesitate to demand the best of each experience before moving on.

Sevens can be materialistic if they set their sights on consuming more of whatever looks appealing, and an Eight wing can intensify that trait. The self-confidence of an Eight lets this Seven decide it's okay to claim a bigger piece, a better seat, a longer stay.

It also helps the Seven buckle down to work more readily, instead of flitting from one half-finished job to another.

Eight's tremendous willpower comes in handy for a Seven who might decide to climb Mt. Everest while it's sunny, but who otherwise might back down when the weather changes. With that extra grit, any area of interest can be followed to the heights of excellence.

The Seven's natural charm becomes more focused with an Eight wing, and this person's determination can help get the most from any experience. Why settle for smelling the roses when you can buy the whole garden? When the dinner is enlivened by so many fun people, why not have the restaurant owner stay open all night? Getting things done is as easy as snapping your fingers.

Sevens Going To One

Ones see things in black and white, while Sevens see infinite shades of gray. But these Sevens *do* have a black-and-white attitude when it comes to comparing themselves with others. Not along the lines of good and evil or right and wrong, but they're always aware of who's having the most fun. And they firmly expect it to be themselves.

The judgmental quality which keeps Ones concerned with constantly doing the right thing, then getting upset whenever they let their high standards lapse, shows up in Sevens who are concerned with making the best choice at all times. They tend to resist being pinned down, but these Sevens won't hesitate to take action when it comes to making their ideals a reality. If they dream of a better world, they won't just stop with dreaming.

In fact, they can become obsessive about getting things done – whether the project is building homes for the poor, or organizing the biggest party their town has ever seen. They'll get impatient with people who don't share their vision, blaming short-sighted outsiders for not jumping on their colorful bandwagon. Worse yet, for insisting on nit-picky rules that miss the big picture.

Still, nobody does a better job of filling a bandwagon with citizens eager to help build homes for the poor than a Seven going to One. For passionate, big-picture service to society, it's hard to find a better combination.

Sevens Going To Five

When a Seven is pressed for commitment, it's easy to retreat into the Five world of considering every option in privacy. These Sevens want to examine every decision, withdrawing into themselves for as long as necessary.

They tend to be more introspective, just as you'd expect from a Five. They also escape the typical Seven aversion to anything painful, because they're good at viewing everything around them with an objective eye. Whether something is painful or pleasurable, right or wrong, is a matter for study rather than for avoidance.

These people want to explore the world, yes, but they don't want to just rack up experiences. Instead they want to rack up knowledge, to understand everything they come across. Consuming is fine, but so is contemplation, and Sevens who go to Five will be masters of each.

Their enthusiasm and creativity makes them both able and likely to contribute something original to the world. They won't just have some brainstorm and discard it ten minutes later; they'll follow it to see where it leads. They might even become pedantic about it, pushing their theories onto other people, but it's a safe bet that they'll pursue any subject of interest into the deepest recesses of the library. A person can't *have* too much knowledge!

TYPE EIGHT

Eights With A Seven Wing

The Seven wing makes these Eights even more sociable and outgoing, even more boisterous and ready to keep the party going all night. It's easy for them to be generous hosts and expansive guests who'll make the most of any crowd. They might talk louder than other people in the room without even realizing it, because they're so wrapped up in the exuberance of the moment.

These people are also more at risk of becoming addicted to food or drink, drugs or danger. They're confident of their own ability to come out on top no matter what risks they take, and eager to explore whatever life has to offer. They love the adrenaline rush that comes with adventure, and they see no reason to hold back on anything.

This can make them extremely successful at new ventures, and they tend to be enterprising visionaries. They might show a strong sense of idealism, or they might be more ambitious for material goods. Either way, they'll go after what they want with no holds barred, and if things go wrong they'll explode in a rage and then simply move onto something else.

Graced with Seven's good cheer, these Eights can be delightfully funny. Their action-oriented bravado comes with a light touch, and their sense of humor makes up for flashes of temperament or moodiness. Want an exciting party guest? Here's your best choice.

Eights With A Nine Wing

Nine's peacemaking skills give these Eights a more mild-mannered quality. They seem almost immune to anxiety, combining an Eight's inherent fearlessness with the Nine's ability to take a long-view perspective on any situation.

Such quiet strength may lead others to look up to this Eight, who usually responds with a benign gentleness. It's as if everyone knows who's in charge here, so there's no need to make a fuss about it. No need to prove a point. The Nine-wing Eight simply takes this easygoing dominion for granted.

More introverted than other Eights, this one may show a dry sense of humor or irony that only a few people get to see. They don't need a large circle of friends, and if they're surrounded by admirers they still like to keep things informal. What's the point in putting on a show?

The only time you'll see a show is if this normally steadfast, patient and kindhearted person feels some deep threat. It takes a lot to get a rise out of someone who seems almost abnormally calm, but a blowup will be hard to forget. The Eight might not even notice the effects of such anger on those nearby, merely returning to a tranquil state with the assurance that everything's just fine now that order has been restored.

Eights Going To Two

Because Twos tend to over identify with those around them, while Eights have trouble identifying with anyone but themselves, this can be a good combination. Being able to see themselves in someone else's shoes makes these Eights more empathetic, more compassionate and more thoughtful.

It also brings out their nurturing instincts – they don't just want to offer protection, they want to offer healing. They'll see more readily how everyone is connected, and extend their trust without waiting to make sure it's deserved.

Of course, this makes them more vulnerable, and they become more likely to take things personally. If you hurt their feelings, they won't forget it.

In fact, they can become a little demanding or dependent or downright obsessive about their loved ones, showing a possessive side that reveals how much they fear any loss.

However, they're also better able to express their fears and weaknesses, which gives them less to be afraid of. Getting in touch with their own gentleness enhances their strength, and this makes them very good communicators. Their concern for others' welfare comes through with no defensive guard attached, and it makes people more willing to open up when the Eight is equally willing to open up and reveal the softness within.

Eights Going To Five

Eights who go to Five are, not surprisingly, more studious and introspective. They're able to step back and take a broader look at any issue, considering its philosophical aspects before blindly jumping into action.

This makes them great at figuring out strategies and systems, but it can also make them more isolated from others. If they start feeling guilty about thoughtless actions, they could wind up brooding...to the point of such deep regret that they withdraw from the world and sit around worrying about defeat.

However, when they take the time to examine their own motivations and allow their more intellectual side to provide insights, they can be strongly coherent thinkers. Their self-reliance extends into the realm of thought as well as the realm of action, and they practice moderation rather than going for all the gusto they can get.

Five's ability to think things through before embarking on a crusade is handy for Eights, complementing their inherent ability to get things done without a whole lot of contemplation. Stepping back from their usual energetic mode of action can give them the time they need to examine questions from a larger perspective... and offer the chance to realize that "thought before action" can be a highly effective way of getting through life.

TYPE NINE

Nines With A One Wing

Any Nine who takes on the traits of a One will display an abundance of common sense. While always aware of what's fair and what's right, this person is likely to be a moral leader who teaches by example rather than by proclamation.

Self-control is exceptionally strong in One-wing Nines, who have very little trouble going along with whatever the rules say to do. They prefer not only upholding the rules, but also prefer going along with the prevailing order, which makes them very cooperative.

They have a keen desire to contribute to the common good, and when this streak of idealism is combined with strong organizational skills, the Nine becomes a valued crusader. However, you might also see them being critical of others and wearing a cloak of self-righteousness.

Whether or not they press their judgments on others, these Nines are outstanding when it comes to integrity. They'll never brag about it, because they're always modest about their own best traits…while at the same time they're quick to notice *your* best traits. Their blend of openness and objectivity makes them a good judge of character.

Nines with a One wing are generally well composed, emotionally controlled people who believe in upholding the highest principles and doing good wherever possible.

Endearing and gentle with others, they have an easy time maintaining their composure…because they know, deep down, that they're doing the right thing.

Nines With An Eight Wing

On the surface a Nine and Eight might seem so dissimilar that it's hard to imagine such a combination. But the combined traits add up to a very solid blend of inner strength and sensuality, good nature and good leadership.

People tend to give in to Eights, while confiding in Nines. So Eight-wing Nines can be amiable leaders, making everyone happy to go along with whatever they decide. And decisions aren't nearly as big a problem for these Nines, because they have Eight's direct, forceful nature to keep them from vacillating too long.

On the down side, they might simply call the shots with placid comfort, never *caring* what anyone thinks. They can be more direct about going their own way, more forceful and assertive, and even callous at times.

But all that is tempered by Nine's gift for identifying with others and making everyone feel understood. So even if people are grumbling about some high-handed decision, they'll usually acknowledge that at least it was announced with the kind of easy, friendly demeanor you can't help but like.

Sensual details are a joy to these Nines, even more than to others. Given the choice of dwelling on mental activity or enjoying material comforts, they'll always go for what feels good.

Nines Going To Three

Threes' ability to take charge of life is valuable to these Nines, who can behave a little more assertively without worrying that their relationships will never survive.

The Nines' tendency toward self-effacement is balanced by the Threes' love of the limelight, making these people far better at staying fully involved with the world.

They're more likely to take control of their own life and less likely to live through others. And, just as you'd expect from someone moving toward Three, there's an admirable productivity, energy, and efficiency in the air.

With such heightened self-confidence comes a willingness to role-play, and Nines can be great at this. They're already good at fitting in with others, so taking on new roles is no big challenge, especially when they share the typical Three ability to cast themselves in whatever light the situation requires.

Connecting with their own vitality can make these Nines even more inner-directed, more focused on their work, and more decisive about their personal goals.

However, it also can make them get caught up in their own image, their own vanity, so they're working solely toward the goal of being admired.

Still, the energy and achievement you expect from a Three provides a nice balance for the Nines' usual laid-back attitude. As long as they're not taking on too much in the hopes of impressing others, they're likely to be far more practical and productive than the usual Nine.

Nines Going To Six

Sixes are massively loyal and faithful to whatever and whomever they've committed themselves to honor. Such deep devotion benefits Nines who go to Six, because it gives them the courage to take on new risks.

Even though risk is inherently distasteful to both Sixes and Nines, when keeping their word involves taking a risk, they'll do it without hesitation. (Or at least without much hesitation.) Once they've committed themselves to a person or a cause, they'll shed their usual tendency to get lost in "make-work" details and instead focus wholeheartedly on their commitment.

With the anxiety that plagues most Sixes, these Nines are even more likely than others to seek relief in the usual sources of comfort – from TV and food to drugs and alcohol to soothing baths and fluffy, cozy blankets.

All Nines know right where to get the best comfort, but those with a Six's sense of anxiety need it even more. It's easier for them to overreact to uncertainty, because the wall of repression that normally hides a Nine's doubt and anxiety is never very strong in a Six.

There's also a tendency to procrastinate, to weigh every possible option before making a decision, and since both types share this trait it's even stronger in Nines who go to Six. However, there's an equally strong tendency toward being honest and realistic…to say whatever needs saying in the most practical way possible.

Laurie Schnebly Campbell grew up in a family that discussed psychology around the dinner table, so her favorite part of writing fiction is creating characters with likable, plausible personalities.

After six novels, including one that beat out Nora Roberts for "Best Special Edition of the Year," she began sharing her techniques with other writers – and fell in love with teaching, both in person and online. In fact, she chose her website name so that groups would find it easy to *www.*BookLaurie*.com* for workshops.

Laurie spends her weekdays writing ads for a Phoenix advertising agency, which is good practice for writing synopses that make people "want to buy the product." She also enjoys playing with her husband and son, recording for the blind at Talking Books, vacationing in Sedona (the red-rock town named for her great-grandmother), and working with other writers.

© Paul Markow

"People ask how I find time to do all that," she says, "and I tell them it's easy. I never clean my house!"

Made in the USA